MANTLES

PAST AND PRESENT

What Mantles Are and How They Work

by

Roberts Liardon

Mantles Past and Present: What Mantles Are and How They Work

ISBN: 978-1-6675-0619-7
eBook ISBN: 978-1-6675-0620-3

Copyright © 2024 by Roberts Liardon

Roberts Liardon Ministries
P. O. Box 4215
Sarasota, FL 34230

E-mail: info@RobertsLiardon.org
www.RobertsLiardon.org

Published by Harrison House
Shippenburg, PA 17257-2914
www.harrisonhouse.com

2 3 4 5 / 28 27 26 25 24

Editorial Consultant: Cynthia D. Hansen
Text Design: Lisa Simpson

DEDICATION

I dedicate this book to Phyllis Mackall, the first person to believe in my call to author books when I was still a teenager and just starting out in ministry. Phyllis was the editor who helped me write my first book, *I Saw Heaven*, which sold more than a million copies in its first year.

Phyllis came to me one day in the mid-1980s and introduced herself; then she began talking to me about the prophetic call on my life and about God's call on my life as an author. She told me that she sensed the same anointing on me to produce books that she had witnessed on Gordon Lindsay and on Kenneth E. Hagin. That first meeting was a remarkable way to make someone's acquaintance.

In the years that followed, Phyllis was also the first person besides my family to pray into God's call on my life to produce books. She was instrumental in helping me write a few more of my first books as I developed in the equipment needed to fulfill that part of my call.

After working for a newspaper out East, Phyllis had served as the senior editor for Pat Robertson. By the time I met her, she was working as the senior editor at Kenneth Hagin Ministries in Broken Arrow, Oklahoma, for several years. Phyllis' heart was always to keep the prophet's words on the printed page true to the way Heaven had spoken those words through him.

This was Phyllis Mackall's gifting — she could spot the prophetic anointing, and she was called to come alongside and help prophets develop in their call to get the prophetic word in print. My friend knew how to listen and how to write.

Phyllis explained to me, "The printed page is a significant part of your call, Roberts. You will come into writing books that will live generationally, so you must be careful that your words on paper reflect the way the Holy Spirit speaks to you."

Back then as a teenager, I didn't fully understand what Phyllis shared with me along this line. But as years passed and I published many more books — especially as I began to write my *God's Generals* books — the meaning of her words became clearer to me.

Phyllis Mackall graduated to Heaven in the mid-1990s. I'm so thankful for her friendship, for her prayers, and for the priceless wisdom Phyllis freely imparted to me that helped launched me into fulfilling this part of my call — as an author in the Kingdom of God.

CONTENTS

PREFACE

Although I grew up around church folks talking about mantles, I never did an extensive study on the subject. However, I believed in the concept, because it was obvious at times that someone had received the mantle and anointing from a person who had moved on to Heaven.

The Pentecostal old-timers I've talked to over the years have had a better understanding of this subject of mantles than many of us "young-timers" do. And I've found that the issue that can often bring some confusion is people's different ways of defining certain Christian terms. In today's church, the words *anointing, impartation, gifting,* and *mantle* are often improperly interchanged or meshed together, which can create misunderstandings about how God operates in the realm of His Spirit. We'll discuss this at length in the pages that follow.

This subject of mantles isn't widely mentioned in the Scriptures, and it's a subject I haven't preached on much throughout my years of ministry. I have a rule I normally follow: What the Bible talks a lot about, I need to preach a lot about. On the other hand, what the Bible talks only a little about, that's how much preaching I should do about that subject. And if the Bible says nothing, I will say nothing.

That's the easiest rule in establishing a good foundation for a good preacher. As for this subject of mantles, it is only a small part of the Scriptures. But even though its part is small, it's a very important subject that we need to better understand, especially as we navigate these last days before Jesus returns.

I believe that's why the Lord recently said to me, *"I need you to preach on this subject of mantles."* Sometimes He expects me to step out of the boat, preach what I know, and believe for the rest. That's what I've been doing, and it's been exciting.

God still wants to highlight this part of His character and His power — the truth that for certain operations and offices, He produces mantles that are supposed to continue to operate in the earth and be generationally passed on.

So I'm writing this book by God's instruction. I understand that what I offer is only a part, not the total picture. But that's what He is asking me to do — to simply bring my part.

In certain aspects of this subject that I'll address, I could say, as the Apostle Paul did, "I speak by permission, not by commandment" (*see* 1 Cor. 7:6). I'm offering my part as thought for consideration. I don't approach this subject like "This is gospel truth and it can't be any other way." I don't believe we're going to have absolutes on every aspect of this subject of mantles, but we're going to fine-tune the question so we can further our understanding and the pursuit can become more accurate.

One thing I want to stress: This book is *not* written for the purpose of helping the reader identify the mantle he or she is destined to receive. Too many start trying to do that in the flesh when I minister on this subject.

The purpose for my writing this book is simply to help bring clarity to the Body of Christ on this subject of mantles. I wouldn't do this if I didn't feel prompted of the Lord to do it. Certain books come at certain timings, and this is a book that is working at this moment. Some teachings are kept until an appointed time when the Body of Christ gets in a position to begin to process it correctly. This may be that moment for this subject.

With all that said, I present this book as my way to put a brick in the wall of understanding mantles. I invite others to please put their bricks on top of mine, and let's help build a wall of understanding. That way we can all learn, and the next generations can reap the benefit — because the day of mantles has returned. It is here. Mantles are an important part of the last-day revival, and there has to come an understanding that can help move the Church forward in preparation for Jesus' soon return!

Dr. Roberts Liardon
Sarasota, Florida, 2024

INTRODUCTION

We're about to take a journey into the world of mantles. I believe the Holy Spirit is highlighting this subject at the present time because there are past mantles that God wants to resurrect, as well as mantles for today that He wants to bring forth fresh and new.

Although not everyone will receive a mantle, everyone can be blessed by them. We all should know what mantles are so that when they show up in a person's life to demonstrate God's power and glory, we can tap into them and receive the impartation God desires to give us.

Mantles are usually granted, with rare exceptions, at the death of the person who carried them because a mantle is meant to represent a lifetime anointing to fulfill a lifetime ministry. Then when that mantle is no longer carried by a living person, it sits quietly in the realm of the Spirit, waiting for the next one who is both called and qualified to inherit it, activate it, and use it to God's glory.

We're about to take a journey into the world of mantles. I believe the Holy Spirit is highlighting this subject at the present time because there are past mantles that God wants to resurrect, as well as mantles for today that He wants to bring forth fresh and new.

Will that person do all that is necessary to qualify for that mantle? Will he or she activate it by faith and obedience and use it to God's glory as He desires? If not, the mantle will just sit there, along with countless unused mantles that have accumulated through the centuries. Some of these past mantles have lain dormant for many years, and God desires to resurrect them.

Awhile back I had a vision along this line. It pertained to a strong apostolic anointing upon a particular ministry.

The man who carried that mantle is still alive, but he's not walking in that anointing as he once did. He left everything behind to go a different direction. To this day, the church in that region is still reeling.

People ask, "How could that minister do it?" In the natural, I cannot put two and two together. I don't know how a person can choose to step down from a ruling apostolic ministry that accomplished so much for the Kingdom of God. For decades, this had been a mighty move and a great ministry — and then this minister chose to step down.

Many people scattered, hurt and disappointed. Some left the faith. For those who had been left to deal with the aftermath, it was a very difficult time.

So in this vision I was talking to the Lord, and I said, "If I could have any anointing, I'd want that one" — and I spoke the man's name. And the Lord said, "Well, go over and get it."

So in the vision I went to this minister's house, which I had visited before in the natural, and began looking for this man's mantle, going through all the closets, all the bedrooms, all the cabinets, every little drawer. I went through the upstairs, the downstairs — I looked *everywhere*, but I couldn't find that mantle. It wasn't inside the house. Where could it be?

In the vision I walked out through the back door and looked around the backyard, but I saw nothing there. Then I walked around to the side of the house, and I saw a pile of backyard trash — scrap lumber and small tree limbs. And in the midst of that pile lay the mantle I was looking for. It had been discarded, thrown outside the house onto that trash heap.

The Lord said to me, *"Many of My mantles are just like this one, lying in trash heaps, and they need to be recovered by authentic pursuers. I'm looking for those who don't just want the fame or prestige that the mantle may bring. They have within them a heart desire to fulfill My purpose for giving the mantle in the first place: to build the Kingdom, win souls, and accomplish the assignment."*

In the vision, I reached down and pulled the mantle out from under the scrap lumber. It was tattered and torn, and it didn't look beautiful the way it did when I had seen it in operation many years earlier — but it was still the mantle. I remember in the vision, I folded it up, put it in my pocket, and began to run home. Then I came out of the vision.

I asked the Lord, "Does this mean I have the mantle?"

I'm still waiting for that answer. I thought, *Well, at least it's in my pocket. I may have to pull it out one day and "strike the water" with it.*

Meanwhile, those words the Lord spoke have been working in me: *"Many of My mantles are just like this one, lying in trash heaps."* There is a sense of urgency in His words.

And so began the assignment of writing this book...

Chapter 1

A Divine Setup

It was 1962, and young Reinhard Bonnke was freshly graduated from the Bible School of Wales and on his way home to Hamburg, Germany. Since he hadn't had an opportunity during his Bible school years to visit London, Reinhard decided to take an extra day to stop in the city and go sightseeing. He purchased a ticket on a touring bus that allowed him to get on and off for the entire day at no extra cost.

After hours of crisscrossing London on the bus, Reinhard got tired of sitting and thought, *I'll just get out and walk down some of these streets to get some exercise.* While walking down one neighborhood street, his attention was caught by the name "George Jeffreys" engraved on the nameplate of one of the homes.

Reinhard stopped. The young man had just learned in Bible school about George Jeffreys, the famous Welsh healing evangelist who operated in an anointing of great healing power, with signs and wonders following. During his lifetime, Jeffreys was also one of Britain's greatest church planters, pioneering more than 100 churches himself. The Elim denomination he founded is still alive and strongly functioning today.

Could it be that the man who brought the gospel of signs and wonders to the United Kingdom lives here? Reinhard thought. *The man whose book I just read? No, it couldn't be — George Jeffreys is a common name. There are thousands of men in the United Kingdom with that name! But could it be?*

Then a voice on the inside said, *You have time to kill. Why don't you find out?*

WHO WAS GEORGE JEFFREYS?

George Jeffreys was a Welshman who got saved, along with some of his friends, during the final weeks of the Welsh Revival before it came to an end in 1905. The young men were frustrated that they had missed the glory days of the revival. They said to each other, "The revival shouldn't end; we just got in it!"

So Jeffreys and his friends made a mutual commitment that no one would get married before revival returned. They would work together to fire up revival again, and only then would they get married. And that's what these young men did. Not one got married till revival was spreading like wildfire through the land once again.

The Holy Ghost revival that started in Azuza Street came to England in 1907, and every member of the group got baptized in the Holy Ghost and spoke in tongues. Revival had returned, and the young men started getting married. Soon everyone in the group had started their families as they worked for God in the revival — all except George Jeffreys, who never married.

He stayed focused in his call, and in the years that followed, he became the great healing apostle.

As previously mentioned, Jeffreys built more than 100 churches himself, and the Elim denomination he founded is still functioning today.

Jeffreys operated in an anointing of great healing power. The most spectacular healing miracle I've read about that God performed through Jeffreys occurred to a man with only one foot who came to his meetings. The man's other leg had only a stump where a foot should be. He was one of the local men, and everyone in this British village knew him.

George prayed for this man that night and told him, "Go buy a new pair of shoes, because in the morning you'll have ten toes." Everyone present thought, *We'll see about this!*

So the man went out after the meeting and obediently bought a pair of new shoes. Thank God, he didn't say, "I already have shoes at home, so I'm not going to spend money buying another pair." If that had been his attitude, the man would have missed his healing, because the working of miracles, one of the gifts of the Spirit, was in operation through Jeffreys on his behalf (*see* 1 Cor. 12:10).

You see, when God gives an order, we're to obey it. If we don't obey, we can abort the blessing or miracle that He is wanting to bring.

I read this man's version of what happened next. He said, "I had a hard time going to sleep that night because I kept waiting for my other foot to show up." Imagine being one-footed all your life, and then a great prophet comes to town and tells you,

"You will have ten toes tomorrow morning." It probably *would* be a little difficult to go to sleep that night!

**When God gives an order, we're to obey it.
If we don't obey, we can abort the blessing or miracle
that He is wanting to bring.**

Somewhere in the middle of the night, the man finally fell asleep — and he woke up the next morning with two feet and ten wiggly toes!

That's the kind of creative miracle I want to see more of in our lifetime!

So the man put on his two new shoes and went walking down the street. And he caused quite a stir! When people saw this man who had hobbled around town for years walking normally, they exclaimed, "What *happened* to you?!" People began to follow the man toward the morning meeting. And when he walked into the big auditorium, which seated several thousand people, the crowd started screaming and wildly praising God. Talk about having a revival meeting that day — that crowd had one! And the spark that ignited the fire was that man with ten new wiggly toes!

That was one of the most unusual miracles that occurred in George Jeffreys' life, but it reflects the power of the healing ministry God gave him.

A SUPERNATURAL CONNECTION

When Bonnke saw that "George Jeffreys" nameplate on the house, all that the name represented flooded him with a sense of inner excitement.

Bonnke walked up to the house and knocked on the door, and a woman answered it. Young Bonnke asked, "Excuse me, Ma'am, is this the home of George Jeffreys, the man God used to bring signs and wonders to Great Britain?"

And the woman answered, "Yes."

Wow, I found George Jeffrey's home! Reinhard thought.

"May I please see him?"

"No." The housekeeper's large frame filled the doorway like a roadblock.

But just as the disappointed young man was about to turn around and leave, a deep voice boomed from the staircase inside the home, "Let him come in!"

Overjoyed, Reinhard politely squeezed his way past the disapproving housekeeper into the house, and there he saw an elderly George Jeffreys slowly making his way down the stairs. The young man was in awe. A few minutes earlier, he hadn't even known that the older man was still alive, and now he was standing in the presence of this great healing evangelist!

"Oh, Mr. Jeffreys, I'm so glad to meet you. I have read your book! I just finished Bible school, and God has called me to preach the Gospel in Africa. I was on my way home to Hamburg and just stopped in London for the day to see the sights. And I was just walking in this neighborhood when…"

But right in the middle of Bonnke's clumsy attempt to explain how he happened to be there that day, Jeffreys sunk down to his knees, pulling Reinhard down on his knees with him. Then the elderly minister laid his hands upon the younger man and began to pray loudly and fervently, blessing Reinhard and petitioning God that what was on his own life would come upon this young man.

After Jeffreys finished his passionate prayer, Bonnke got up off his knees and said, "Thank you. I believe that now my Bible college is complete. I've earned my degree, and I've received my anointing from George Jeffreys." After a warm farewell, Reinhard left to get on the train and head on to Germany. When he arrived the next day, his father picked him up at the train station and said, "Son, I've got some sad news. We just heard that George Jeffreys died last night."

Reinhard cried, "Oh, this can't be! I was just with Mr. Jeffreys yesterday! But I believe a connection took place while I was there. And I believe I caught a mantle!"

A divine transfer had indeed taken place. In the years following when Reinhard talked about his time with George Jeffries, Bonnke would explain, "God's anointed are interconnected from generation to generation, and God connected me to the former generation's healing evangelist for *this* generation. These things do happen, and it goes right back to the Apostle Paul! It goes right back to Jesus Himself!"

Chapter 2

WHAT IS A MANTLE?

Reinhard Bonnke would go on to become one of the world's most renowned healing evangelists of our time. So what was it that Jeffreys possessed and transferred to Bonnke? What is a mantle, and what is contained in it?

A mantle is a supernatural "cloak" that God places on a person of His choosing to accomplish a task of significant importance and that normally flows generationally. A mantle resides in the realm of the Spirit and rests on that individual as a lifetime assignment in order to execute an essential part of God's plan.

When that person's time on earth is over, a divine transfer of assignment often takes place. When that happens, it becomes evident to those who are observant that what was upon one person now rests upon another of a new generation.

First, let's look at a dictionary definition for a literal mantle. A mantle is defined as *a loose, sleeveless garment, cloak, or shawl, similar to a cape or a wrap, that a person wears to protect from the outside elements.*

We see in the account of Elijah and Elisha that the mantle is referred to as a garment that came from Elijah (*see* 1 Kings 19:19; 2 Kings 2:13). It was a piece of Elijah's clothing, most likely his outer garment that he wore for warmth and for protection from the elements.

In military terms, a chain mantle might also be worn on a soldier's chest as a form of plated armor for protection.

The word *mantle* can also refer to *an important role, responsibility, function, position, capacity, task, or job that passes from one person to another.* The verb form of the word *mantle* means *to be clothed, cloaked, or enveloped in.*

**A mantle is a supernatural "cloak" that God
places on a person of His choosing
to accomplish a task of significant importance
and that normally flows generationally.**

In Reinhard Bonnke's case, he didn't leave with a piece of George Jeffreys' physical clothing. So if the actual cloth was required for the transfer of Jeffreys' mantle to take place, then Bonnke missed it. After Jeffreys prayed for him, the younger man should have grabbed the older minister's coat and taken it with him!

But Reinhard Bonnke didn't miss it. The transfer of Jeffreys' mantle took place in the spiritual realm — and on the other side of that divinely orchestrated encounter, Bonnke knew he was a different man.

We're not talking about the transfer of a physical cloth here. The passing of Elijah's mantle to Elisha was simply a natural manifestation of a spiritual reality. A transition took place as a generational prophetic assignment was transferred from the elder prophet to the younger. We'll discuss this spiritual transaction at length in later chapters.

So what is a spiritual mantle comprised of? It is actually a multifaceted function, an invisible "cloth" made up of different threads. Those threads represent a combination of several dimensions, interwoven to supernaturally work together within a mantle as a "full-package deal."

The passing of Elijah's mantle to Elisha was simply a natural manifestation of a spiritual reality. A transition took place as a generational prophetic assignment was transferred from the elder prophet to the younger.

One of those threads is the job description, or the calling, of the person ordained to receive the mantle. That job description involves not only the calling of the one who carries the mantle in the present generation, but also a blending of the callings of those who carried that mantle in past generations. The call attached to a mantle is a duty that the possessor of the mantle is sent to accomplish in the earth.

Other threads woven into the mantle are divine mandates, or assignments, that the one carrying the mantle is sent by God to fulfill. The threads of a mantle also include giftings, such as the nine gifts of the Spirit, anointings, and impartations that the mantle carrier must be equipped with and operate in to fulfill that call.

CAN A MANTLE BE DIVIDED?

In most cases, we see a mantle passed on to a single individual. However, sometimes it is difficult for one person to carry all that is encompassed in a particular mantle, so it's possible that more than one might carry different aspects. It's not that there are two or three mantles on a person's life; there is one. But in rare instances, one mantle may be divided between two to carry the full scope of its assignment.

Take George Jeffreys' mighty call, for example. His ministry included both great healing evangelism and church planting, so his mantle was one that had a multifaceted function.

But Bonnke never pioneered a church. The part of Jeffreys' mantle that Reinhard Bonnke received was the healing evangelism function. All that Bonnke's ministry accomplished over the decades that followed with the huge crusades and the mass healings represented an increasing of the healing mantle that rested on the man named George Jeffreys.

This was in line with Kingdom principles, for God always moves from glory to glory (*see* 2 Cor. 3:18). Likewise, when a mantle transference takes place, it shouldn't diminish in the next generation but only expand in power and influence.

So what about the church-planting function of Jeffreys' mantle? Well, as a church historian who has studied the out-working of mantle operations over the years, I've come to a conclusion that's relevant in this case. I believe it's possible at times for a mantle that has rested on a person to be transferred to a corporate body of believers, rather than on one individual, when the mantle carrier passes away.

In the case of Jeffreys, Bonnke received the powerful healing evangelism side of Jeffreys' mantle. But I believe the church-planting, ministry-birthing function of his mantle actually fell upon the last church he preached at — Kensington Temple.

At one time, the large majority of full-Gospel churches in London had a relationship with Kensington Temple. It was a mantle with that kind of significance. Every leader of that church to the present, along with their congregations, has worked in the power of that mantle and helped plant more than 150 churches throughout the surrounding region.

I'll conclude this brief discussion on the definition and nature of a mantle with an important point to remember as we explore this subject further: Mantles aren't as broadly distributed as many think. I do believe that relatively few people in the Body of Christ carry a mantle, and as you read on, you'll see why I say that. Yet everyone needs to understand what a mantle is so they can recognize its operation on the earth and receive blessing from it.

Now let's continue to explore the world of mantles. There is so much more to understand and discover!

Chapter 3

'UNTANGLING THE THREADS'

Understanding this subject of mantles can be a challenge when working with believers within different circles of the Church. Especially in Pentecostal and Charismatic circles, *mantle* is a term that we often use without understanding it as well as we need to. Our Christian verbiage sometimes interchange *anointings, impartations, giftings,* and *mantles* as if they referred to the same spiritual realities, yet all four refer to something different.

Too often in certain circles of the Body of Christ, people choose "buzz words" that make people feel happy; yet they're not always correct in the way they use those terms. When that is the case, those individuals will have to wake up somewhere down the road and realize that their view of what they may have received needs to be adjusted — that it doesn't actually match the status or grandeur of the term they have been using.

The word *mantle* is simply used too loosely in the Body of Christ.

I often have someone come up to me and say something like, "I had a prophetic word spoken over me that I have the mantle of Kathryn Kuhlman." When I hear a comment like that, I don't buck it or argue with the person. I realize it is most likely simply a misunderstanding of terms.

The truth is, there are entire camps in the Body today that have mixed up their Christian verbiage so much that a person can't trust a lot of what they are saying. People will call different spiritual experiences this or that, using different terms like mantles, anointings, impartations, visions, dreams, and encounters — and they will think they are right in how they use all those terms. But there is a danger in this trend, because these terms can become buzz words without biblical moorings — and in the process, lose the power of their actual scriptural intent.

For instance, to inherit a mantle is to receive an assignment from Heaven that lasts a lifetime. So if someone who is still running his own spiritual race says he is passing on his mantle to you, you can know that is not what is happening. That person may be blessing you with an impartation, but it is not a mantle.

Different terms like mantles, anointings, impartations, visions, dreams, and encounters can become buzz words without biblical moorings — and in the process, lose the power of their actual scriptural intent.

You can receive an impartation of a spiritual gift or an anointing from a man or woman of God, and that spiritual substance will be present and working in your life. If you'll cultivate what has been given to you, it will become part of you as you pursue God's plan and purposes, and it will flow through you to bless others. However, this doesn't mean you received the mantle of that person.

Some people have a legitimate encounter with a minister in which a spiritual gift was imparted to them or an anointing came upon them by the Spirit. After the encounter, it's possible that others are able to then spot at times certain aspects of that minister's particular anointing in these people's lives.

But then too often wrong assumptions are made. "That person must have So-and-so's mantle." I get a little nervous with that kind of comment because, as I said, believers don't keep the Christian vocabulary very policed. Too often people mix anointings, mantles, and impartations together; yet each word is distinct from the other terms.

So let's try to "untangle the threads" and clear up the confusion between these terms that tends to muddle the issue when talking about mantles. What *is* the difference between an anointing, an impartation, and a mantle? Getting this answer straight will help set you up to think right and be correctly positioned to receive all that God desires to bless you with as you pursue His plan for your life.

ANOINTINGS

Given this confusion of terms that prevails in the Church world today, I want to give you descriptions and examples of two of the primary terms in our discussion: *anointing* and *imparta-tion*. Later in Chapters 13-16, we will discuss an example of a multi-generational *mantle*.

Let's begin with *anointing*. The Hebrew word for *anointing* comes from the Greek word *chrio* and carries the meaning of *smearing*, or the free application of oil. When used symbolically of the Holy Spirit, the word *chrio* means in part *to consecrate* or *to appoint*. It also refers to the burden-removing, yoke-destroying power of God given to an individual to accomplish a sacred task.

Author and Bible teacher Rick Renner, an authority in New Testament Greek, explains this concept of applying the oil of anointing in his first volume of *Sparkling Gems From the Greek*:

> The word "anoint" that is used primarily in the Old Testa-ment Septuagint and the Greek New Testament comes from the Greek word *chrio*. This word originally denoted *the smearing or rubbing of oil or perfume upon an individual....* Technically speaking, the word "anoint" has to do with the rubbing or smearing of oil on someone else.... I refer to the anointing as a "hands-on" situation. It took someone's hands to apply the oil.
>
> Let's consider this concept in the context of God anointing our lives. God Himself — the Great Anointer — filled His hands with the essence of the Spirit and then laid His mighty hands upon our lives, pressing the Spirit's power and anoint-ing ever deeper into us. So when we speak of a person who is anointed, we are actually acknowledging that the hand of God is on that person. The strong presence of the anointing that we see or feel is a signal to let us know that God's hand is personally resting on that individual's life.[1]

---

[1] Rick Renner, *Sparkling Gems From the Greek* (Tulsa, OK: Teach All Nations, 2003), p. 363.

In the Old Testament, the oil was used to signify the transfer of the anointing of God to consecrate and make holy for His work and His purposes. We see this in the account of Moses anointing Aaron for the priesthood.

And he [Moses] **poured some of the anointing oil on Aaron's head and anointed him, to consecrate him.**

Leviticus 8:12 NKJV

The anointing oil is used as a symbol of the anointing of the Holy Spirit, which is activated by a person's faith and transferred in the unseen realm under both the Old and the New Covenants. Spiritually, this word *anointing* refers to the ability and presence of the Holy Spirit working through a human vessel to equip and empower that person to accomplish God's purposes.

Rev. Colin Dye, my long-time friend and colleague who pastored Kensington Temple in London for 31 years, offered me this clarifying definition of the "thread" called "anointing":[2]

To be anointed means to be equipped with the divine capacity and ability to perform a sacred task. It implies both *authority* (the right to act in a certain way or to perform Heaven's tasks) and *power* (the ability to carry out those tasks). The Holy Spirit's power (ability) must be put into action. Then His operative power is released and becomes effective, producing results that are felt, seen, heard, or experienced.

One of the most common means of transferring an anointing is through the recipient closely following another's ministry. A person who faithfully follows a particular minister or ministry

---

[2] Personal correspondence from Rev. Colin Dye of Colin Dye Ministries, https://colindye.com.

often receives a measure of the anointing that God has placed upon that minister.

Spiritually, this word *anointing* refers to the ability and presence of the Holy Spirit working through a human vessel to equip and empower that person to accomplish God's purposes.

Rick Renner's definition of *anointing* helps clarify what's taking place in this ongoing spiritual process that I sometimes call "picking up an anointing." We could say that the more a person follows and receives from a particular minister, the more opportunity "the Great Anointer" has to lay His hands upon that person's life and "press in" a measure of the Holy Spirit's anointing that rests upon that minister.

I can share an example from my own life in which I received an anointing from a minister — in this case, Rev. Kenneth E. Hagin. I heard Brother Hagin preach more than any other preacher in my life, and his ministry has blessed our family and my ministry more than I can express. I am forever indebted to Kenneth E. Hagin for the price he paid to teach the message of faith to his generation.

When I was a young boy, I lived three miles from Brother Hagin's Bible school in Broken Arrow, a suburb of Tulsa, Oklahoma, and my family would regularly attend his meetings. Grandma discovered Brother Hagin in the late 1960s when he was just starting out in the Tulsa phase of his ministry. She had heard about this minister but didn't know much about him.

But Grandma was like Dr. Lester Sumrall in that she would ride every wave of the Holy Ghost as it rolled in, no matter what she had to go through to get there. And from the time she attended her first Kenneth E. Hagin meeting, Grandma was hooked. Our whole family started attending all of Brother Hagin's meetings that we could through the years.

So if you watch me or listen to me preach, you can see at times the anointing I picked up from Brother Hagin. It will sometimes manifest when I'm preaching.

I have an anointing from Brother Hagin, but I don't have his mantle. By being around him and receiving from his teaching and his ministry for all those years, that anointing came upon me, and I have kept it and cultivated it. I so appreciate that anointing. I have picked it up by sitting under and receiving from his ministry for so many years. It's a part of my DNA; it's part of who I am.

THE NATURE OF IMPARTATIONS

I've found that there are many people who think they have the mantle of some great person of faith, but in actuality they do not. They may have an impartation from the supply of a person's spirit that is real and legitimate, but that isn't a mantle.

As I mentioned earlier, in the world of a mantle, there are anointings, giftings (which include fivefold ministry offices and the nine gifts of the Spirit), and impartations. All of these are encompassed in a mantle, but the reverse cannot be said. A mantle is not simply an element of the giftings or the anointing upon a person's life.

So let me give you my definition of an *impartation*. The word *impartation* is a functional term denoting an authoritative transaction in the Spirit — through laying on of hands, through words spoken by the Spirit, etc. — in which a person receives spiritual giftings and equipment needed to fulfill God's purposes.

The substance deposited in your spirit from an impartation stays and resides in you so you can operate out of what was received as you learn to yield to the Holy Spirit's promptings. We can see an example of this kind of spiritual transaction in the Apostle Paul's words to his spiritual son Timothy:

> **Therefore I remind you to stir up the gift of God which is in you through the laying on of my hands.**
>
> **2 Timothy 1:6 NKJV**

We also see an example of this kind of authoritative transaction in Numbers 27, where the Lord conferred upon Joshua a measure of the honor and authority that was upon Moses as leader over Israel before it was time for Moses to depart.

> **The Lord said to Moses, Take Joshua son of Nun, a man in whom is the Spirit, and lay your hand upon him; and set him before Eleazar the priest and all the congregation and give him a charge in their sight. And put some of your honor and authority upon him, that all the congregation of the Israelites may obey him....**
>
> **And Moses did as the Lord commanded him. He took Joshua and set him before Eleazar the priest and all the congregation, and he laid his hands upon him and**

commissioned him, as the Lord commanded through Moses.

Numbers 27:18-20,22 AMPC

Also, we see an example of an impartation of a spiritual gift operating in Peter and John's ministry. The two apostles traveled to Samaria to minister to those who had been born again but were not yet filled with the Spirit. When they laid their hands on the people, an immediate outward sign of that impartation — the infilling of the Spirit — occurred.

We know from other scriptures that the people began speaking in other tongues as they were filled with the Holy Spirit (*see* Acts 2:4, 10:46, 19:6). The power demonstrated in that spiritual transfer of anointing even caused the resident sorcerer who observed what had happened to ask the apostles to give *him* whatever the Samarians had just received (*see* Acts 8:18-19)!

The word *impartation* is a functional term denoting an authoritative transaction in the Spirit in which a person receives spiritual giftings and equipment needed to fulfill God's purposes.

An impartation denotes a more specific and authoritative spiritual transfer than what I just described as picking up an anointing from a minister that you might closely follow over a substantial period of time. In addition, the spiritual giftings and equipment you receive through impartation will continue to work *in* you, not just flow *through* you.

For some, when the Holy Spirit comes upon them, they act like the one from whom they received an impartation. For others, they do a measure of the work of that person, with the impartation manifesting more in certain displays of God's power rather than on a regular basis.

Rev. Colin Dye also offered to me this definition of an impartation, which I thought was an excellent addition to our discussion:

> When we speak of impartation, we usually mean the effective working of the anointing — the "felt impact," or the power of the Holy Spirit.
>
> We impart a spiritual gift (Rom. 1:11) by operating with the Spirit — teaching, healing, prophesying, etc. We can also impart by activating a spiritual gift in another. (*See* 2 Tim.1:6, where Paul imparted "the gift of God" to Timothy through the laying on of hands. Either Timothy received the Holy Spirit this way, or some ability of the Spirit was activated in Timothy by Paul.)
>
> This is the difference between anointing and impartation. The anointing is the presence of the Spirit and the authority to operate in His power. Impartation is the effective operation of that power according to the will of God. It is the flow of the Holy Spirit's power that achieves a specific supernatural result.[3]

WIGGLESWORTH'S IMPARTATION TO LESTER SUMRALL

Let me illustrate an example of a spiritual impartation by sharing an account along this line from the life of one of God's generals — Dr. Lester Sumrall.

---

[3] Ibid.

I came to know Brother Sumrall when I was a young minister. In fact, my spiritual father was first Lester Sumrall and then also Oral Roberts. God orchestrated my life so beautifully to land in those two worlds and to be with all the right people at the right time in the right place when I was starting in the ministry as a teenager.

When Lester Sumrall was a young minister, he traveled around the world with a man named Howard Carter, a minister who is best known for being the man who brought great revelation to the Church regarding the gifts of the Spirit.

As a young Englishman during World War I, Howard Carter was drafted by the British government. So he went to plead his case before the tribunal, telling the officials, "I cannot shoot Germans because I love the German people and have many German friends."

The tribunal told Carter, "If you won't go to war, you have to go to prison." So Howard spent the war doing hard labor in prison.

But Carter was allowed to take his Bible with him, so after returning each day from working at the hard-labor camp, he would study the Bible at night in his cell. And during the years Carter spent in that cell, God gave him the revelation of the nine gifts of the Spirit and how to teach that subject to the Church.

Carter later wrote a book entitled *Questions and Answers on the Gifts of the Spirit*, which remains a classic teaching on that subject. Still today, most Pentecostal and Charismatic ministers' teaching on the gifts of the Spirit is based on Howard Carter's book — because what Carter taught is correct.

It was in the 1930s when Lester Sumrall was in his 20s that God supernaturally connected him with Howard Carter, and for years they traveled around the world together, preaching the Gospel. They returned to England during the beginnings of World War II, just as it was starting to rumble.

Sumrall kept hearing about a Englishman named Smith Wigglesworth, who had earned quite a reputation by then as a faith preacher who had seen multiple notable miracles in his ministry. Wigglesworth was also known for his abruptness at times in how he'd pray for people. He didn't demonstrate that abruptness in every service, but he did it frequently enough that it lives as a part of his legend. And Smith's personality and his gruff manner worked for him. I don't know if it would work for you. But that was just how Wigglesworth was, and it worked for him — and God used him mightily.

So when Sumrall arrived in Great Britain, he wanted to meet the man he had heard so much about and read of in the Christian magazines of his day. And when he did meet Wigglesworth, the elder minister said to Sumrall, "I've been reading about your travels with Howard Carter." (Sumrall was a writer and would write articles for Christian magazines about his journeys around the world.)

So Wigglesworth asked Brother Sumrall, "Would you come preach at my Easter convention?"

Young Sumrall thought, *This is great. I don't get to just see Brother Wigglesworth; I get to preach for him and eat with him!*

Sumrall later relayed this experience personally to me. He said, "I got up to preach and had gone on for 45 minutes or so when I felt a big hand on my shoulder. I turned around, and it was Brother Wigglesworth. He said to me, 'The Holy Ghost finished about 15 minutes ago — when are you going to finish?' I replied, 'Right now!'"

So Sumrall finished in short order, and later that evening Wigglesworth extended an invitation to him. He told the young man, "You can visit me anytime you like," and gave Sumrall his home address in Bradford, England.

Eventually Lester Sumrall decided to go visit Wigglesworth. Years later Brother Sumrall personally related his first visit to Brother Wigglesworth's home to me. He said, "I looked like an Englishman."

Young Lester wore a bolo hat that many recognize as the Charlie Chapman hat, and he carried an umbrella and a folded newspaper. He took the train from London to Bradford, walked down the street, and knocked on the door of Brother Wigglesworth's house.

Wigglesworth was a big man. When he opened the door, his body filled the whole frame of the door. And there stood Wigglesworth — perfectly dressed, every hair in place.

Lester said, "Good morning, Mr. Wigglesworth."

Wigglesworth replied gruffly, "What's underneath your arm?"

"An umbrella and newspaper."

"Well, I don't allow lies in my home."

Young Sumrall stuttered, "Oh, excuse me, sir." Turning, he ran to some nearby bushes and stuck the newspaper in the bushes; then he returned to Smith's front porch, where his host said, "You can come in now."

Sumrall told me, "That was the strangest visit I've ever had with any person in my life."

Wigglesworth said to Sumrall, "Sit down and let me read you the Bible." Then he read a few chapters from the Bible and said, "Now let's pray." Once they finished praying, Wigglesworth said, "Let me read you some more."

All morning long, Smith went back and forth like that between reading the Bible and prayer. Then his daughter Alice said, "Dad, lunch is ready."

So the two went to eat lunch, during which Wigglesworth talked about just a few other topics besides prayer and the Bible. Finishing his meal first, he said, "I'm tired now. Come back if you want. Have a good day; it was nice to see you again." And he walked out, leaving Lester to finish his lunch alone.

Brother Sumrall later told me: "As I left Brother Wigglesworth's home for the train station, I thought, *This was the weirdest visit I've ever had to any person's home in my life! I don't know if I want to come back.* I got on the train, but halfway back to London, I found that I had something in me that wasn't there before. And I thought, *I like that!*"

So Sumrall kept going back to visit Wigglesworth over the few years that he lived in England before the war. The day came, however, when he received a letter in the mail from the British government — an official notification that all foreigners had to leave. The Battle of Britain was about to begin, and the British government didn't want to have to deal with the safety of non-citizens during the time of crisis that was at hand.

So as Lester was saying goodbye to all of his British friends, he traveled to Bradford to tell Brother Wigglesworth in person what was happening. Lester took the same train, walked down the same street, and knocked using the same door knocker — and this time, Smith simply said, "Come on in." Lester had learned how to properly visit Wigglesworth's home: namely, with no newspaper!

Brother Sumrall later related to me what happened next. "As we stood in the foyer, I said, 'Brother Wigglesworth, I must leave. I have to say goodbye today. It's my last visit for a while.' We spoke briefly about Hitler and the battle that was on the horizon for Britain.

"Then before we even went into the parlor, Wigglesworth laid his hands on my shoulders. As he did, such power came through him to me that I dropped to my knees. Smith prayed and cried, his tears flowing down his cheeks and onto my forehead. And in his prayer of blessing, Smith said this: *Father, give unto him a portion of my spirit of faith.*"

Sumrall told me that from that day forward for the rest of his life, fear left him and faith consumed him. You can see from this example that these kinds of spiritual impartations are supernatural transactions with portions and anointings that are given and granted.

If you had known Brother Sumrall, you would recognize that some of his gruffness came from that Wigglesworth impartation. However, my understanding is that Lester Sumrall did not receive the Wigglesworth mantle.

Wigglesworth laid his hands on my shoulders.
As he did, such power came through him to me that I
dropped to my knees. And in his prayer of blessing,
Smith said this: *"Father, give unto him
a portion of my spirit of faith."*

According to historical records, that mantle has likely never been picked up. Yet there have been people who received impartations from Brother Wigglesworth, and the greatest example of this category that I am aware of was Lester Sumrall. I could tell at times when it flipped from Lester Sumrall to what Brother Wigglesworth prayed over him — that portion of Smith's spirit of faith — as I watched Brother Sumrall preach.

If you didn't know about that impartation, you might think, *I don't like it when Brother Sumrall is gruff like that.* But when I'd see that side of him, I got happy and thought, *Oh, there it is!*

I knew what to look for. Sumrall had received a spiritual blessing from Wigglesworth through what we call an impartation, but I don't believe Sumrall received the Wigglesworth mantle. Too often we throw all those kinds of terms together, but they are each distinctly different.

You may be inspired and strengthened by one of these ministers whom God used so mightily, and there may be a certain degree of their grace or their anointing that has found its way upon your life and within your spiritual equipment. That is a powerful addition to your life in God, but that is not a mantle.

You can receive an anointing or an impartation from someone and not have the mantle of that person.

LESTER SUMRALL'S IMPARTATION TO ME AS A YOUNG PREACHER

I'll continue this particular thread on spiritual impartation by sharing my own story of the impartation I received as a young preacher from Lester Sumrall when he was in his latter years.

Let me emphasize at the outset that I am *not* setting myself up as the inheritor of Dr. Sumrall's mantle. The context of this part of our discussion is to define an "impartation" as it differs from the definition of an anointing or a mantle.

Remember, the word *impartation* denotes an authoritative spiritual transfer of giftings and equipment necessary for fulfilling God's purposes. The substance of an impartation is something that stays and resides in a person so he can operate out of what he received as he learns to yield to the Holy Spirit's promptings. I am forever grateful that I received this kind of impartation from Dr. Sumrall during those years I was blessed to know him.

Lester Sumrall eventually became my spiritual father. The first time I actually met him, I was preaching in Sweden in the late 1980s. I had seen Brother Sumrall preach several times at our church in Tulsa, so I knew who he was. I had shaken his hand once, which I counted as a great day. I had also read his books, and I appreciated his ministry. Then in Scandinavia, we found ourselves ministering at the same conference.

I got up to preach my afternoon session, and in walked Lester Sumrall to sit and listen to me preach. In my youthful insecurities, that was intimidating! But I was already on stage, reading my scripture text when he walked in. So I preached to the side of the auditorium where he wasn't sitting so I wouldn't have to look at him!

After the meeting, I found myself in the lunchroom sitting with Lester Sumrall and the host. Brother Sumrall looked at me and said, "I've heard about you."

My mind started racing. *I wonder what he heard?*

He continued, "I came this afternoon to see if it was true."

I wanted to ask, "And?" But Brother Sumrall never explained further, so I was left to wonder whether or not he had come to a positive conclusion.

I came to another conference session that evening, and as Brother Sumrall and I were walking out afterward, he said to me, "Tomorrow we shall have breakfast together."

He didn't ask me; he just told me. But I was smart — I just answered, "Okay, what time?"

"When the restaurant opens, about 8 o'clock or so. I will be there, and you should be there too."

Well, I was scared to death because I thought, *What am I going to say to this man?* I respected him so much, but I was intimidated.

When you're going to meet greatness, remember — you can't be sloppy, so prepare yourself and look your best.

I got up early, showered, freshly shined my shoes, made sure my shirt was pressed, and put on my tie and jacket. I looked like I was ready to go preach.

I was downstairs 30 minutes early for our breakfast meeting. I found the woman who was in charge the restaurant and said, "I want this table, and please put nobody else around us." And when those elevator doors opened at 8 a.m., I was standing there, ready to say good morning to Brother Sumrall.

Here's a side note: How you approach greatness determines the depth to which you may gain something in that encounter, so look the best you can. Don't be casual about it. If you're casual, you won't get much.

Also, when you're around greatness, cooperate. Don't sit there trying to show off your low-level intelligence. Be humble, be receptive, and plan on writing down notes. Let God bless you through the divine opportunity He has set up.

When Brother Sumrall walked out of that elevator, I was ready on the outside — but so nervous that I was scared spitless! We sat down, and it was like an interview. He asked me all sorts of questions.

"You said you went to Heaven. Is that true?"

I said, "Yes, it is."

"Well, that's wonderful. It's scriptural. People have been allowed to see Heaven..."

And so the conversation continued, and Brother Sumrall kept talking all throughout breakfast. Then he said, "I live in South Bend, Indiana. You should come see me. I'm done now.

Bye." And with that, Brother Sumrall got up from the table and walked off!

**When you're around greatness, cooperate.
Let God bless you through the divine opportunity
He has set up.**

I was left sitting there alone, thinking, *Well, that was weird.*

I was raised with social skills. I was raised to believe that manners matter, that there are certain ways one is to do certain things. And that's true.

Brother Sumrall didn't have some of the manners I was taught about while growing up. He was a man who even in casual conversation was commanding, and he could seem abrupt. But that was just his personality and his apostolic nature. He always used to say, "I'm Irish; I'm old; I'm apostolic; and I'm taking care of 3,000 preachers. So sometimes I'm kind of grumpy." If you had all of that going on in your life, you might be a little grumpy at times too!

But that morning, I just thought, *Well, that was an interesting visit. I'm glad that at least I was able to have a nice breakfast with Brother Sumrall.*

I didn't take seriously what he had said to me right before he left: "I'm in South Bend; come and see me." I didn't think it was a true invitation. I just thought it was a polite way to say goodbye.

ACCEPTING DR. SUMRALL'S INVITATION
TO HIS 'HOME TURF'

But Brother Sumrall's secretary was one of my ministry partners in those days. About four months later, she called me and asked, "Roberts, when are you coming to South Bend? Brother Sumrall keeps asking for you."

I said, "I didn't know I was supposed to come."

"Did he tell you to come?"

"Yes," I replied, "but I just thought Brother Sumrall meant it as a nice thing to say when he was saying goodbye. I didn't think he was serious."

"He only says what he believes and what he means," the secretary replied. "I can't cover for you anymore. You've got to get up here, or you're going to get in trouble."

Well, I didn't want to be in trouble. And I did *not* want Brother Sumrall to be mad at me! So I took a flight that next week and flew to Chicago. Then I got on a vibrating little plane that flew me to South Bend, and I rented a little car to drive the last few miles to his office. I arrived at his headquarters, and they brought me into his office about 10:30 in the morning.

I said, "Good morning, Mr. Sumrall!"

"Nice to see you; have a seat."

He sat at his desk, and I sat down in a chair.

Brother Sumrall looked at me and then asked, "What's your first question?"

"I don't have any questions," I answered. "I thought we were just going to have a conversation."

"Don't ever come to my office and waste my time again," Brother Sumrall said. "Always have questions."

Well, my brain immediately began to formulate questions! They weren't the best questions, but at least they were questions — so I survived that first South Bend meeting with Dr. Sumrall.

Then he said, "Let's go have lunch."

I thought, *Praise God, we can get out of this office!*

We had a good time visiting at lunch, and afterward we went back to his office, where Brother Sumrall said to me, "I think we're done today."

I thought, *Praise the Lord!* At that moment, I just felt relieved that our time together was over.

Dr. Sumrall said, "Let me bless you before you go. Would you like me to bless you?"

"Oh, yes, I want to be blessed," I replied.

I was taught as a kid to collect prayers and blessings. My grandmother and mother always made me and my sister get in every prayer line we could to take advantage of every opportunity to get prayed for.

So being a Pentecostal, I've learned how to flow with any type of prayer person who came along over the years. Some shake you, some hit you, some rattle you, and some knock you over and then jump on top of you! All kinds of things happen, so I was ready for whatever Brother Sumrall wanted to do as I walked around his desk and got on my knees in front of him as he sat in his chair. I expected a good Pentecostal session, and I was ready for it!

But Brother Sumrall simply grabbed my forehead between his third finger and his thumb and said, "Be blessed! You can go now."

I thought, *That was the weirdest prayer I've ever received in my life.*

Later as I got on the plane, I thought, *I am never going back. That is the strangest thing I've ever been a part of, and I'm not going to do that again. I'll just sit in the crowd, listen to Brother Sumrall preach, and read his books. But I don't want to eat with him, and I don't want to visit him again.*

Then the Spirit of the Lord spoke to my heart and said, *"Actually, this was the first of many."*

I wanted to bind those words — but you can't bind Jesus! You just have to submit.

I answered, "I don't want to, Lord. I went to Brother Sumrall's office, and it was nothing but weirdness. He rebuked me in the first ten minutes because I didn't have any questions. And then he just yelled, 'Be blessed! You can go now.' What kind of prayer is that?"

I continued, "Why are You asking me to be around Brother Sumrall? I know You have used him really wonderfully throughout his life, but he is gruff and seems to be a grumpy-ish type of person."

The Lord said to me, "*There's a reason you feel so unfit in Lester Sumrall's presence. When you're with greatness, that person's strength, accuracy, and stability confront everything inside of you that needs to be adjusted during that encounter. And what begins to shake and vibrate in you is what has to be healed, fixed, and realigned.*"

The Lord continued, "*Write down everything you are feeling as you speak with Dr. Sumrall. Then work on a few of those things until the next time you go back. When you return, see if you still shake or feel bad in those areas. If you do, you still have a ways to go. If you're doing better, you'll notice it.*"

In this way, I learned how to have the uncomfortableness of greatness work for my benefit.

That's also part of what one called to be a mantle carrier has to do during his time of training. Most will run from a person who makes them uncomfortable because they don't know the first step of relating to him. But the one called to carry a mantle has to press in to the uncomfortableness of training.

Approximately two hours into my flight back home from visiting Dr. Sumrall, I discovered a spiritual deposit in me that I didn't have in me before that trip. I thought, *Aha! I did get something!*

Through all my nervousness and mishaps in that first meeting, I still received an impartation in the realm of spiritual giftings for my call. That "something" grew over time, becoming a powerful addition to my spiritual equipment, and Lester Sumrall and I became close friends. As I'll explain further later, he also filled the role of spiritual father in my life during his latter years on this earth — an honor I hold as a precious privilege to this day.

**The one called to carry a mantle has to press in
to the uncomfortableness of training.**

Brother Sumrall was a world apostle, but his days of miracles and of building and establishing works had taken place earlier in his life. I got to know him at the end of his apostolic life during his giving years. He told me, "I'm getting ready to leave the earth, so I need to give out what I have to the young people."

I didn't witness all the power and miraculous display of Lester Sumrall's earlier seasons. I heard about it, and I saw the fruits of it. All of that was very real, but I wasn't there when it was happening. But today I carry within me an impartation of God that I received from Lester Sumrall, and I'm eternally thankful for it.

Chapter 4

THE OPERATION OF MANTLES IN THE NEW TESTAMENT

In the next few chapters, we're going to explore what Scripture tells us about the passing of a mantle in the Old Testament case of Elijah and Elisha. But before we do, I want to address this question: *How is the operation of a mantle manifested in the New Testament?* And we have to start with this understanding: Everything from the Old Testament has to come through the Cross before it touches us, and that includes this spiritual transaction of receiving a mantle.

First, we know that Galatians 3:27 (NASB) says, "For all of you who were baptized into Christ have clothed yourselves with Christ." That word *clothed* is a mantle word, and we see that each new believer receives this Christ mantle the moment he or she accepts Jesus as Savior and Lord. This is the greatest mantle that can be carried on the earth today, and it sits upon every one of us who has been born again.

We are all clothed with the mantle of Christ, which is the indwelling Holy Spirit, the corporate anointing shared by the entire Body of Christ. However, the Body of Christ is also called to be clothed with the *power* of the Holy Spirit. Jesus told His disciples, "…Behold, I will send forth upon you what My Father has promised; but remain in the city [Jerusalem] until you are *clothed* with power from on high" (Luke 24:49 AMPC).

**Everything from the Old Testament
has to come through the Cross before it touches us,
and that includes this spiritual transaction
of receiving a mantle.**

We are clothed with a greater measure of the mantle of Christ when we are endued, or clothed, with spiritual power (*see* Acts 1:8). No one who believes in Jesus is excluded; all are eligible by right to receive the baptism in the Holy Spirit and to operate in the power of the mantle, or the clothing, of Christ. This gift of the Holy Spirit enables us to do signs, wonders, and miracles — in other words, to do the works of Christ. All believers are eligible to receive this mantle of Christ.

But we can't discard the idea of mantles operating under the New Covenant in the way we see them in the Old Testament, because they do exist. We can still find mantle assignments on the earth today. These are key operations that continue under the New Covenant, but without the same dependency of God's people on the one who carries the mantle.

Yet although these specific mantle assignments do exist and operate in the Body of Christ in this day, they are given to a relative few. Meanwhile, everyone else can learn to recognize and benefit from the ministries of those appointed to carry these mantles so that God's plan can be furthered and His purposes fulfilled.

OPERATING WITH ACCURACY IN THE SPIRIT REALM

I want to add a crucial principle to help us stay on track as we go forward in this discussion of spiritual mantles and their operation on the earth.

The principle is this: Learning to operate correctly in the spirit world is a requirement for all ministers — and certainly it is an imperative for those who are called to be mantle carriers. *The one who is called has to build the kind of platform that a mantle can sit on.*

You see, the spirit world has three categories of citizens in it: God and His angels, Satan and his demons, and mankind — the human spirit. These three are the only kinds of spirit entities that occupy the spirit world.

The one who is called has to build the kind of platform that a mantle can sit on.

The spirit world is never quiet; there is always activity. However, not all of the activity in the spirit realm is of God; some is demonic. And it's the human presence in the spirit world that has to decide which side he or she is going to yield to while operating in that unseen realm.

God created a spiritual law — for us, not for Him — that His Word and His spiritual manifestations agree. What you read in the Bible, the Holy Spirit performs today for you and me. Whatever the Holy Spirit does can be found in direct line with the principles of the Word. These two agree, and we are to live between these two borders in our spiritual life and activity.

Now, there is activity in the spirit world outside of these boundaries, but it's not how God told us to function spiritually. He said that we are to operate only between the borders of the Word of God and the Spirit of God.

So if what you're preaching cannot be found in the Bible, then you need to seriously consider the possibility that you should stop talking about that. If your encounter cannot be confirmed by Scripture, it is possible that 1) what you experienced was an illegal function of a wrong spirit; or 2) it is a religious, euphoric feeling or product of your imagination that your carnal mind created to stay in charge of you.

Those who are called to the ministry must choose to live their lives in the spirit world *God's* way. Too many want spiritual activity going on all the time. But the Holy Spirit doesn't operate according to people's desires or expectations!

I've been in meetings where I've gotten up to preach and have known what God wanted me to do. At the same time, I could sense what the crowd wanted.

In those kinds of situations, you have to decide whom you're going to obey. Sometimes if you do what the Lord says, the crowd isn't going to invite you back. They're not going to like you, and your offering is going to be small. I'm just being honest.

So you have to decide in that moment the kind of Christian and minister you will be. Will you do what the Lord wants done in that moment, no matter what it may cost you in the natural, to be honorable to Him and to His heart for His people?

**Those who are called to the ministry
must choose to live their lives
in the spirit world *God's* way.**

Now, some people aren't willing to do that. They are scared that if they don't do what the crowd wants, they'll lose their ministry.

If that's you, let me say this: Maybe you *should* lose your ministry. Or maybe you don't actually have one — at least until you change how you operate in your ministry.

There are ministers in the prophetic and Charismatic camps who need this kind of counsel — not to destroy their ministries, but to fine-tune them and to better position them to produce gold and not brass.

By that, I mean it's possible for ministers to be operating in the Spirit and then, if they're not seeing the outward manifestations they want to see, to lean into the wrong side of the spirit realm without knowing they're doing it. When that happens, people receive a mixture instead of a purity of what God's Spirit intended to demonstrate in that instance. That mixture causes weakness and other demonic traits to begin to be seeded in people's hearts — poisonous seed that will germinate and grow over time.

We can see this kind of spiritual mixture manifesting more and more in the Body in this generation. For instance, many prophetic people exalt their spiritual encounters above Scripture. Others will try to make the two equal. But both are illegal functions in the Kingdom of God. This is never how a believer is to walk out his or her life in God.

I can revisit my past spiritual encounters with the Lord, but I can't hang out there. I hold the Word above all else, and I require every spiritual encounter I ever experience to produce for God without bending the Scriptures to make it work. Either it is scriptural, or it isn't.

Sometimes people ask me, "Are you telling me that the experience I had was not of the Lord?"

Possibly. I will certainly take every spiritual dream, vision, and encounter I hear about and hold it to the plumb line of Scripture! And because I do that, I sometimes become a person's enemy because I threaten his or her chosen reality.

Many years ago, I was preaching at the midweek service of a Pentecostal pastor in New York. I was with him in his office before the service, and I asked him, "What have you been preaching on?"

I hold the Word above all else, and I require
every spiritual encounter I ever experience
to produce for God without bending the Scriptures
to make it work. Either it is scriptural,
or it isn't.

You can learn a lot quickly in 10 or 15 minutes if you just ask a pastor what he or she has been preaching on. I've learned to do that as a matter of course when I preach at another minster's church.

In this instance, the pastor's answer shocked me. He replied, "I've been preaching on the books of Enoch."

I said, "Did you say *the books of Enoch?* I thought there was only seven or eight verses about Enoch in the Bible."

"Well, Enoch is in the Bible," the pastor replied.

"But how do you know that Mr. Enoch wrote those books?"

"Well, it feels right."

Well, you know," I said, "you can feel right eating that third piece of pie and then have that third piece kill you the next week! You should be careful."

This pastor was taking up sacred time in the pulpit to preach out of a text that is not part of the Scriptures because he thought what he had read was interesting. He got angry with me when I didn't agree with his choice of topic and never invited me back — but I was right in my counsel.

All this pertains to building the kind of platform that a mantle can sit on. My counsel to ministers, especially those called to carry a mantle, is this: What the Bible speaks a lot about, you do the same. What the Bible speaks a little about, you do the same. And what the Bible doesn't talk about at all, you do the same.

It's a very simple, powerful, ministerial truth that every minister would be wise to obey. It is so simple that many prophetic people miss it because they're trying to get the next new "heavy revelation" ready.

Preach the Word. Win souls. Pray for the sick. Minister hope for the hopeless. If a revelatory utterance in line with God's Word comes forth, praise the Lord. But don't try to be "deep." People who do that and who always want to talk about their newest revelation become pathetically weird and spooky instead of relevant and powerful the way that the biblical prophets and many historical prophets have been throughout time.

Preach the Word. Win souls. Pray for the sick.
Minister hope for the hopeless. If a revelatory utterance
in line with God's Word comes forth,
praise the Lord. But don't try to be "deep."
All this pertains to building the kind of platform
that a mantle can sit on.

That's one of the reasons I'm writing this book on understanding mantles. I want to help the Body, and particularly those called to the ministry, to make the needed adjustment in this area so we all can be relevant, powerful, and spiritually *precise* and *scriptural* as we each pursue God's plan for our lives in this generation.

Chapter 5

Preparation for a Mantle: Pursuit

So how does one called to receive a mantle stay on track in the time of preparation? What are the prerequisites that a person must fulfill to qualify for such a weighty assignment?

God lays out some key principles in Scripture that help answer these questions through the account of the prophets Elijah and Elisha in 1 and 2 Kings. We're going to see how three primary factors play a key role in preparing the one called to inherit a mantle:

1. Close *association* with the mantle carrier.

2. Staying in the *environment* in which that minister lives and operates.

3. Receiving the constant *influence* of that minister.

A Key Prerequisite

All three of these factors can't be fulfilled with a casual approach. They all require an intentional, sustained pursuit.

Consider this: All the sons of the prophets knew Elijah's departure was near, but only one pursued their leader to the end (*see* 2 Kings 2). Folks can know things by the Holy Ghost, but it is the *pursuit* of what they know that tells the story.

You can know that a deeper place in prayer is available to you but not take advantage of it. Unless you take the time to get alone with God and work with Him, you'll never get there.

Folks can know things by the Holy Ghost, but it is the *pursuit* of what they know that tells the story.

You can know there is an anointing available to you to equip you for what God has called you to do. But unless you purposefully develop your ability to work with that anointing through faith, prayer, and obedience, you'll never obtain it.

Jesus said if you knock, it will be opened. If you seek it, you'll find it. If you ask for it, it will be given (*see* Matt. 7:7). He was speaking of *pursuit*.

We can see this principle in action in the way the call of God came to Elisha, the one chosen to one day succeed Elijah as the number-one, most prominent prophet of that day.

So he [Elijah] departed thence, and found Elisha the son of Shaphat, who was plowing with twelve yoke of oxen before him, and he with the twelfth: and Elijah passed by him, and cast his mantle upon him. And he left the oxen, and ran after Elijah, and said, Let me, I pray thee, kiss my father and my mother, and then I will follow thee. And he said unto him, Go back again: for what have I done to thee?

And he returned back from him, and took a yoke of oxen, and slew them, and boiled their flesh with the instruments of the oxen, and gave unto the people, and they did eat. Then he arose, and went after Elijah, and ministered unto him.

1 Kings 19:19-21

This was a very unusual way for a call to come to someone, but such things do occur in God's Kingdom. So let's dig a little deeper into the spiritual principles that are revealed in this passage.

When Elijah cast his mantle on Elisha, something triggered in the younger man that got his attention and caused him to move toward the prophet. Verse 20 says, "He left his oxen out there in the field and *ran after* Elijah...." The pursuit had begun.

Elisha said to Elijah, "...Let me, I pray thee, kiss my father and my mother, and then I will follow thee. And he [Elijah] said unto him, Go back again: for what have I done to thee?" (v. 20).

When Elijah cast his mantle on Elisha,
something triggered in the younger man
that got his attention and caused him
to move toward the prophet.

The prophet Elijah was walking down the road that day by divine instruction. The Lord had told Elijah that Elisha was to be his successor (*see* 1 Kings 19:16). As Elijah approached, this young man was out doing his chores, focused on plowing with the oxen, when he happened to look up, and there was the man of God! Then Elijah did something the younger man wasn't expecting — the prophet threw his mantle on Elisha and then kept walking on down the path.

As Elisha watched Elijah walk away from him, an inward pull was triggered in the young man he had never experienced before — to the point that Elisha pursued the prophet and asked him to wait for him. In other words, Elisha was saying to Elijah, "Stop — wait right here on this tree stump; don't go anywhere. Let me go back and say good-bye to my mom and dad, and then I'll come and follow you!"

Elijah answered in essence, "Do what you wish; I'm not making you do anything." And Elijah just kept right on walking down the path.

So Elisha returned to the world he knew. And if that was Elijah presenting him with a test to see what was first in his life, Elisha didn't take long to pass the test! He killed two of his oxen — necessary to his present livelihood — boiled their flesh, and gave the meat to the people to eat. That was Elisha's "point of no return"; he was saying good-bye to his former season.

HEAVEN'S PROCESS OF SUCCESSION

Let's look again at the key moment described in First Kings 19:19 "...And Elijah passed by him, and cast his mantle upon him." In that single act, Elijah signaled God's intent: that one day

Elijah's mantle — his anointing, his prophetic office, the spiritual deposit that God had given him — was to be passed on to Elisha.

Elijah's mantle was a governmental mantle — one that was equal to the powers of the time. Elijah had the ability to control weather, to confront governments, and to move things the way they should go. So this was a great mantle that God wanted in the earth, and Elisha was to become his successor.

Knowing how to follow is important in every person's walk with God. But when it comes to what is required to receive a mantle, it is essential — and it is usually a long pursuit. Scholars say that Elisha likely served Elijah for ten or more years of his life, although it may have been somewhat shorter or longer.

Bottom line, qualifying for a mantle takes time and involves an intentional pursuit, even though the person must be first called to receive it. Normally, it's a lifetime relationship of commitment established in the heart of the younger toward the senior.

At times the senior minister selects a successor, but the younger person isn't willing to pay the price required. In that case, the senior must continue in prayer and in performing the works of God. If later the mantle assignment captures the attention of the younger, it will cause him or her to begin to pursue a closer relationship with the senior minister, and the divine process of discipling the next mantle carrier can then commence.

An internal desire begins to grow in God's appointed successor for the mantle that rests upon the elder: *I want that. I'm willing to pay the price for that.* It's not just an emotional fleeting of a moment.

Everyone else might get bored with or weary of following mantle carriers, but the true disciples remain intrigued with them. When everyone else forgets them, the disciples are still saying, "I'm here, and I'm not leaving you." Something holds them beyond any emotional attraction. There's a spiritual union forming, and it takes time.

**Bottom line, qualifying for a mantle
takes time and involves an intentional pursuit,
even though the person must be first called
to receive it.**

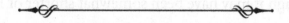

My Personal Pursuit

I learned the importance of pursuit as a young minister in my relationship with Dr. Lester Sumrall. I knew there was more to learn about how God called him and what He sent him to do. And I was a pursuer — I wanted to know all of it.

I was listening for what this general had learned each step of the way and the revelation God gave him through the years. I had learned my lesson the first time I visited Brother Sumrall in South Bend. So from then on, I'd always have some questions already prepared when I came to visit. And I'd pray, "Lord, give me the opportunity and environment that allows me to ask these questions and get some answers."

In my meetings with Brother Sumrall, I'd sometimes start out with easy, shallow questions but would always be working toward deeper questions — and we'd eventually get there. Brother Sumrall might start the conversation by asking where I had been ministering recently and what subjects I had been preaching on. But soon I'd say, "Dr. Sumrall, I have some questions," and he'd say, "Okay, pull out your yellow pad." (He humorously called me "the man with the yellow pad who always has questions.")

I'd have 15 or 20 questions written down, just to make sure I had enough "ammunition" for my time with Brother Sumrall. I'd ask my first question, and that's usually all it took to get some momentum going.

Those private sessions with Brother Sumrall produced some very interesting discussions that were a vital part of my spiritual growth as a man and a minister. As I'll explain in more detail later, Lester Sumrall became my spiritual father. I'm so thankful I accepted his invitation to learn from him, but it required an intentional, sustained pursuit on my part over a period of years.

SERVING WITH A SERVANT'S HEART

So we see that pursuit is a very important prerequisite in the obtaining of mantles. Once again, let me emphasize that a mantle seems to come on the person called to receive it when he or she faithfully and intentionally:

1. Pursues both God and the carrier of the mantle.

2. Closely follows and associates in unity with that ministry.

3. Stays in the environment and constant influence of that minister so that whatever is needed can be observed, imparted, or "caught."

In our scriptural example, we see it was Elisha's pursuit that positioned him to receive Elijah's mantle (*see* 2 Kings 2:6-14). We'll talk more about that later.

I need to add a note here, because there is a reality that should be acknowledged: For a variety of different reasons and circumstances, this type of close relationship between the younger successor and the elder who carries the mantle may not be possible. We can see an example of this in the account of George Jeffries and Reinhardt Bonnke in Chapter 1. Later we'll see more examples as we look at the different generations of those who carried the top American healing mantle.

Yet even then, God provides a way to make up for a successor's inability to pursue a face-to-face relationship with the one who carries the mantle.

The one called to inherit the mantle will have pursued and cultivated a covenant relationship with *God* over time, allowing trust in that relationship to be built to a measure of great strength. And along that person's journey in God, a connection in the Spirit will develop with the previous ones called to carry the mantle, coupled with a deep inner hunger to produce God's will on the earth during the present generation.

First Kings 19:21 goes on to define Elisha's new season of pursuit: "...Then he arose, and went after Elijah, and ministered unto him."

Notice it doesn't say Elisha ministered unto the Lord directly; it says he ministered unto the man of God — unto the prophet Elijah. That means Elisha assisted Elijah, serving him in whatever capacity was needed and without a predetermined time limit to his service.

We sometimes call a person in that function *an armor-bearer*. To be an armor-bearer is a position of honor in God's Kingdom, but there are many filling that position today who have the attitude, *How long do I have to do this?*

It's what I call "the second-man itch."

There is an anointing on this armor-bearer function to come alongside and help ministers in any way needed so they can better fulfill their assignment. God will set individuals in that position, and for some, that is to be their call for life.

If our part fits that description of "assistant for life," we might be tempted to say, "Well, I don't want to play that part." Yet whatever we do for the Lord is as the Holy Spirit wills (*see* 1 Cor. 12:11).

To be an armor-bearer is a position of honor
in God's Kingdom, but there are many
filling that position today who have the attitude,
How long do I have to do this?
It's what I call "the second-man itch."

Isaiah 1:19 (NKJV) says, "If you are willing and obedient, you shall eat the good of the land." Some folks may be obedient, but they're not willing to do what God has asked of them. They don't want to fill this type of assistant position because in their minds, being second is less important. Yet in the mind of God, every position is equally important and powerful, and those called to assist another will receive their reward just as much as if they were Billy Graham!

So you have to become Kingdom-minded to fit and function in the Kingdom. You can't bring a secular Western mindset into God's Kingdom and start operating church and ministry that way.

I like the way the Bible says it: Elisha "...ministered unto him" (1 Kings 19:21). Elisha wasn't paying his dues until Elijah died so he could get the older man's mantle. That wasn't the younger man's motive.

If that kind of secular mindset slips in, you'll start entertaining thoughts like, *How long do I have to serve this person?* Yet when God looks at you, He sees the position you're occupying as no less important than the position occupied by the leader you're assisting — because you're obeying what God anointed *you* to do.

**You have to become Kingdom-minded
to fit and function in the Kingdom.**

What is "second-man itch"? It starts with a person thinking, *How long do I have to be number two? I can do it better. If I were on top, I'd do it like this...* That's the itch starting! You better apply some spiritual calamine lotion and fix it fast!

"Well, if I were you, I'd do it this way."

When you start talking like that, you can know that you've taken your eyes off what God has set in front of you. Now you're gazing at what you don't understand and do not have the authority, anointing, or experience to accomplish. You've started to get "itchy."

The Honor of Serving

As we'll discuss later, there came a time in the lives of Elijah and Elisha when the elder prophet was taken off the scene and Elisha stepped into position as the greatest prophet in the land. Years later when Judah was threatened by external enemies, the king asked, "Is there no prophet we can inquire of?"

> **But Jehoshaphat said, "Is there no prophet of the Lord here, that we may inquire of the Lord by him?" So one of the servants of the king of Israel answered and said, "Elisha the son of Shaphat is here, *who poured water on the hands of Elijah.*"**
>
> **2 Kings 3:11 NKJV**

Notice that the way Elisha was described to the king was in terms of *how he had served Elijah*. That is the serving requirement that must be fulfilled prior to the reception of a mantle. And it means serving not just in the public forum, but in the private arena where no one sees.

It is the willingness to do the mundane and the unapplauded because it is in your heart to do it. It is your honor to do it. It is something beautiful to you, and it doesn't matter what your actions say to anyone else. There is simply a heart desire born of relationship to serve.

Many times people try to draw near to ministers who carry some influence or fame for what they can get out of them. There has been an epidemic of that showing up in ministry circles over the past generation. People who fit that description are looking for a way to help themselves progress to the next step in their own ambitions rather than to selflessly serve the minister and learn the ways of Kingdom operations.

It is the willingness to do the mundane and the unapplauded because it is in your heart to do it. It is your honor to do it. There is simply a heart desire born of relationship to serve.

That's why we have a shortage of great American Christian leaders right now. Many of those whom God has appointed for these critical positions have been sidelined. Too many developed an appetite for the world's stupidity and assumed that what they learned from the secular world would work in the church — but it doesn't.

The culture of the world may change, but God's Kingdom remains the same. So we have many in the younger generation who want a mantle and will pay any cheap price for it. They try to collect anointings the way that little boys collect marbles. After a while, they have a bag of anointings but no authentic ministry, because they haven't learned to serve.

The greater manifestations of God's power sit on the back of the servanthood of your life. If you cannot serve joyfully, you will not walk in great power. If you have not learned the beauty of servanthood, you are not qualified to be a great general or to carry one of these rare and weighty assignments we call mantles, even if that call rests on your life.

God watches to see if the person called to receive a mantle is willing to serve without recognition or applause. He wants to know if that person will serve simply because it's right — and if he or she will do it joyfully. If the answer is yes to both, a great mantle will eventually rest on that person, because he or she has demonstrated a servant's heart.

The greater manifestations of God's power sit on the back of the servanthood of your life.

AVOIDING THE PITFALL OF FAMILIARITY

Because a mantle is pursued over a long period of time, the successor and the mantle carrier normally develop a close relationship. This type of closeness is a wonderful blessing, but it brings with it a concern. If both parties aren't careful, a long-term relationship of serving and closeness can breed an issue with familiarity.

Those who walk in this position of servanthood must never allow a time to come when they don't esteem their spiritual leader for who he or she is in God. They must maintain a posture of honor and respect, even if they see or hear things that tempt them to become judgmental or to think less of their leader. If they don't have the personal self-discipline and the spiritual maturity to avoid that pitfall, they disqualify themselves as potential candidates for a mantle.

The same principle applies to those who serve in a local church. Sometimes as people start serving in a church, they get close to the senior or the assistant pastor. Then after some time of serving, the ones serving might become offended or angry with their leader because they've allowed familiarity to creep in. They have lost the correct posture of honoring their leader, no matter what they see, hear, or feel.

**Those who walk in this position of servanthood
must never allow a time to come
when they don't esteem their spiritual leader
for who he or she is in God.**

Preachers have to live the Word just like anyone else. The only difference between ministers and laypeople is this: Not only do ministers have to *live* it, but they also have to *preach* it. So when those called to serve ministers see them struggle at times in dealing with their own lives, they can't let their awareness diminish the way they honor their leaders.

If you cannot process the humanity of Christian leaders, don't get close to them. To be effective in helping leaders, you must accept the fact that they have to work through issues with their marriages, their children, their finances, and their practical responsibilities the same way any other believer does. You're a potential liability unless you understand that being anointed to minister doesn't exempt preachers from having to live by faith, resist the devil, and do everything else all Christians have to do to navigate this earthly life victoriously.

**When those called to serve ministers
see them struggle at times in dealing with their own lives,
they can't let their awareness diminish the way
they honor their leaders.**

I've been around the ministry since I was 17 years old and have known a large number of the world's great preachers. I learned early on that when you get close to leaders, you'll see the "warts." You'll see the difficult moments. And you have to be careful, because when you follow those in leadership positions closely, you can pick up on their mistakes and weaknesses. At that point, you want to ensure that you neither judge them *for* their weaknesses nor imitate them *in* their weaknesses.

CLOSE ASSOCIATION

It has always been interesting to me that all the sons of the prophets knew it was time for Elijah to leave, but only one pursued to the last moment. Only one refused to leave the side of the prophet.

Elisha was the only one who was determined to pass over the Jordan River with Elijah. And because Elisha stayed close, he was at the right place at the right time to receive the elder prophet's mantle.

Let's look at this biblical account of a mantle being transferred from the elder to the disciple.

And it came to pass, when the Lord would take up Elijah into heaven by a whirlwind, that Elijah went with Elisha from Gilgal. And Elijah said unto Elisha, Tarry here, I pray thee; for the Lord hath sent me to Bethel. And Elisha said unto him, As the Lord liveth, and as thy soul liveth, I will not leave thee. So they went down to Bethel.

And the sons of the prophets that were at Bethel came forth to Elisha, and said unto him, Knowest thou that the Lord will take away thy master from thy head to day? And he said, Yea, I know it; hold ye your peace. And Elijah said unto him, Elisha, tarry here, I pray thee; for the Lord hath sent me to Jericho. And he said, As the Lord liveth, and as thy soul liveth, I will not leave thee. So they came to Jericho.

And the sons of the prophets that were at Jericho came to Elisha, and said unto him, Knowest thou that the Lord will take away thy master from thy head to day? And he answered, Yea, I know it; hold ye your peace. And Elijah said unto him, Tarry, I pray thee, here; for the Lord hath sent me to Jordan. And he said, As the Lord liveth, and as thy soul liveth, I will not leave thee. And they two went on.

And fifty men of the sons of the prophets went, and stood to view afar off: and they two stood by Jordan.

2 Kings 2:1-7

We see a progression here in this last journey of Elijah and Elisha. First, as Elijah prepared to leave Gilgal on the way to Bethel, he told Elisha that he was free to stay behind; he didn't have to accompany him. But Elisha refused to stay behind, knowing that Elijah was preparing to go. He wouldn't leave the side of the one he had served for many years.

Elijah left Bethel to travel on to Jericho, where the same thing happened again. Elijah told Elisha he could stay behind, but Elisha refused.

Elijah then traveled on down to the Jordan River, and the same thing happened again when he told Elisha to stay behind. Elisha would *not* leave Elijah's side.

What about the sons of the prophets who also knew that Elijah's time to leave was near? Verse 7 tells us how they positioned themselves: "And fifty men of the sons of the prophets went and stood to view afar off...."

Those who look on from a distance with a pair of binoculars receive nothing but entertainment!

When a desire is produced in your heart, when certain gifts and anointings have provoked you to move toward something God wants you to have, you have to *pursue it* and *draw close.* This is a spiritual law that is imperative for every believer — but it is critical in the preparation process of someone who is called to carry a mantle.

When the desire is something God put there, it doesn't fade away because it goes beyond human want. A human desire may last a few years and then fade, but if it is a desire of the Lord, it could last a lifetime. And in a person's untiring pursuit of that desire, he may find that when an Elijah starts telling him, "You can stay behind," he has the disposition that refuses to relax his hold. Something within that is born of the Lord causes him to cross through that border and keep on pursuing!

You see, the mantle requirement is not just knowing about the chariot of fire. *It is the pursuit that positions the successor to receive the mantle when it falls to the ground.*

Go pick up the mantle if you know with all certainty it is your divine assignment to fulfill. But withhold your hand until you count the cost of it. There's a good bit of work involved, and the commitment lasts a lifetime.

It is the pursuit that positions the successor
to receive the mantle when it falls
to the ground.

Chapter 6

THE TRANSFER OF THE CALL

Finally, Elijah and Elisha reached the Jordan River. It was the appointed destination where Elijah would perform his last miracle — striking the waters of the Jordan River with his mantle and causing the waters to part so they could cross on dry ground — and then transition from this earthly life.

> …And Elijah took his mantle, and wrapped it together, and smote the waters, and they were divided hither and thither, so that they two went over on dry ground. And it came to pass, when they were gone over, that Elijah said unto Elisha, Ask what I shall do for thee, before I be taken away from thee.
>
> And Elisha said, I pray thee, let a double portion of thy spirit be upon me. And he said, Thou hast asked a hard thing: nevertheless, if thou see me when I am taken from thee, it shall be so unto thee; but if not, it shall not be so.
>
> And it came to pass, as they still went on, and talked, that, behold, there appeared a chariot of fire, and horses of fire, and parted them both asunder; and Elijah went up by a whirlwind into heaven. And Elisha saw it, and he cried, My

father, my father, the chariot of Israel, and the horsemen thereof. And he saw him no more: and he took hold of his own clothes, and rent them in two pieces.

He took up also the mantle of Elijah that fell from him, and went back, and stood by the bank of Jordan; and he took the mantle of Elijah that fell from him, and smote the waters, and said, Where is the Lord God of Elijah? and when he also had smitten the waters, they parted hither and thither: and Elisha went over.

2 Kings 2:8-14

This was the moment that the mantle and call of Elijah came upon Elisha. Such divine transactions transpire supernaturally, with giftings and anointings granted as equipment for the assignment.

But let's go back again to the response that triggered the transaction. Elijah asked Elisha in verse 9, "What shall I do for you?" And the younger prophet answered, "Give me a double portion of your spirit."

Elisha wasn't asking for a double portion of Elijah's human spirit. He was asking that a double portion of the anointing of the Holy Spirit and power working in Elijah's life would be transmitted to his life to help him fulfill his own call as successor to Elijah's ministry.

'YOU ASK A HARD THING'

With that in mind, let's revisit what Elijah's response was to Elisha when the younger prophet made that profound request for a double portion of Elijah's anointing.

And he said, Thou hast asked a hard thing: nevertheless, if thou see me when I am taken from thee, it shall be so unto thee; but if not, it shall not be so.

2 Kings 2:10

There is a reason Elijah said, "You have asked a hard thing." Receivers of mantles are taking on a very uncomfortable path in their lives. Along that path is a lack of indulging their own personal will.

Remember, a mantle is a specific and strategic spiritual "cloak" that comes upon a person to fulfill an assignment that God wants to keep working in the earth. Therefore, those who are called to be successors of mantles must come to realize that their personal dreams for their lives will hold very little weight from this point on, because they are picking up divine assignments that have been active on the earth for a while.

Receivers of mantles are taking on
a very uncomfortable path in their lives.
Along that path is a lack of indulging
their own personal will.

When a mantle comes over onto a successor, that person is responsible to carry that mantle to his or her generation and to do whatever is required to function in its power and anointing in order to set people free. This means that the successor's lifestyle, and possibly even his or her personality, must change and adapt to the divine assignment. The mantle has to fit on the person who has received the call.

Today so many people talk about "my purpose, my passion, my dream in life" — and that's what it is. It's *their* emotionally desired passion and purpose.

People who fit in that category wouldn't be willing to make the changes God requires or allow Him the amount of time that is necessary to inherit a mantle. If they could choose to stay "in training" just long enough to receive the anointing and an impartation, they'd be happy. But those who will actually qualify have to do the time.

You don't find the purpose of God by how much you get excited about something. You find the purpose of God for your life in the place of prayer as you *die to self*. You place yourself on the altar as a living sacrifice, and you give up all your personal desires and ambitions. You say to the Lord, "I live for You. Whatever You want me to do, I will do. What is Your bidding, Father?"

This is true for all believers, but it is especially true for those in pursuit of a mantle assignment. The cost is far beyond what most people ever comprehend.

**You find the purpose of God for your life
in the place of prayer as you *die to self*.**

That's why Elijah said to Elisha, "You ask a hard thing" — not an impossible thing, but a hard thing. Part of the hardness is what is required to qualify for a mantle.

Those called to inherit a successional mantle usually go through a process in which they eventually realize that the borders are much tighter and the requirements are more defined than for those who have an individual anointing and calling. Successors actually receive as their own the calling that is resident within a mantle. It's a calling shared with those who came before, and it will be shared with those who inherit the mantle in future generations.

That means those who inherit a mantle have to come to terms with seeing their own aspirations — what they personally have desired for their lives — dissolved in the light of "this is how it's going to be from now on." Certain things that they have dreamed of doing in life and ministry will likely be completely knocked off the plate if they accept the assignment God is calling them to receive.

Dying to Self Required

This is the cost of saying yes to such an assignment, so there has to be a compelling within the person that draws him or her toward it. There is a "deep calling unto deep" (*see* Ps. 42:7), an attraction of spirit, that develops between the disciple and the mantle carrier.

That drawing of the disciple's heart gets his or her attention, and then the spiritual significance starts working in the disciple's heart. This is the process of dying to self, and it is part of the reason it takes time for the one called to be the successor to receive it.

**There is a "deep calling unto deep,"
an attraction of spirit, that develops
between the disciple and the mantle carrier.**

Normally modern believers don't want to talk about dying. They want to talk about "my purpose" and "my big deal in life." But that is what has gotten the modern American Church off track. The focus of too many Christians is selfish — it's full of "me, me, me."

But we don't want you; we want *Him*. We don't want your ambition; we want Jesus' purpose fulfilled *through* you. And you're not going to get that until you die to your flesh and your selfish desires. As long as *you* are alive, the purpose of God for you will not find its force, its strength, and its working authority *through* you.

Someone would walk up to Kathryn Kuhlman and ask, "Kathryn, what's the secret of your ministry? How does the ministry of healing work through you so powerfully?"

And Kathryn would have one answer: "I died. Kathryn Kuhlman died."

"Yes, but how did you get your anointing?"

So people would hear Kathryn's answer, but they wouldn't truly *hear* what she was saying. Yet she told people all the time the secret of the unusual power she consistently walked in. "I died. I know the place; I know the hour; I know the spot where I died. And before every miracle service, I die a thousand more deaths."

Today most people, even those who have a strong call on their lives, are not carrying powerful anointings, let alone a mantle. There is simply too much of *them* still alive.

But God will not anoint you in your flesh. He only anoints you as a sacrifice. *So if you want fire, be a living sacrifice.*

The problem with most of us is that we crawl off the altar, go do what we want to do for a while, come back for a short visit on the altar, and then crawl off again to do our own thing. In that kind of situation, serving God isn't a lifestyle; it's an isolated event defined by our own fleshly preferences and desires.

But when you look at the lives of generals like Ms. Kuhlman and Brother Oral Roberts, you see that it was a daily lifestyle that they lived, not just something they did once. They died *daily*.

God will not anoint you in your flesh.
He only anoints you as a sacrifice.
So if you want fire, be a living sacrifice.

Kathryn would say, "The day I died, I found the greatest power in my life. The power of the Holy Spirit came upon me in the moment that I died."

People would watch the miracles that took place in Ms. Kuhlman's services and say, "I want Kathryn Kuhlman's mantle." If you're one of those people, you need to know this: The first thing you have to do to even get close to it is *die!*

Others say, "I want Brother Wigglesworth's mantle." They read about the manifestations of God through Wigglesworth's ministry — the miraculous healings, the raising of the dead — and they think, *Wow! I want that anointing.* But most of the time, those who say that don't even know what Smith Wigglesworth's life was actually like.

How did Smith Wigglesworth live? Well, for one thing, he got up every morning and danced before the Lord in his night-clothes before he did anything else. Then he took Communion before he even got dressed.

Those were the first things Brother Wigglesworth did every morning. And throughout the day, he'd go no more than 15 or 20 minutes without reading a scripture or saying a prayer. He was continually building his faith. That's the way he lived. So if God draws your heart toward the ministry of someone like Wigglesworth, pursue a deep understanding of the life this general lived that attracted God and caused the fire of the Lord to continually burn in his life and grow ever brighter over time.

That's why Elijah said, "You've asked a hard thing." He didn't say it was impossible. He said it was *hard.* Another way to say that is to carry the responsibility of a mantle, you have to live a restricted life.

There are certain things some Christian leaders do that are not necessarily wrong but that you cannot do if you're a leader called to carry a certain authority or a certain presence of God's anointing. And unless you're willing to die to your desire for those things, that authority and anointing you have carried will not remain.

A restricted life is required to carry the anointings, impartations, and mantles of God, and you have to understand the cost. There is what I call the basic cost, and then there is a unique price for each type of gift. Each may operate a little differently and demand a certain type of cost from the minister that is different than for others. It doesn't make the minister better; it's just different.

For instance, if God is leading you to pursue the type of mantle Oral Roberts carried, you have to know that in his tent meeting days, he would go to his hotel room at about two o'clock every day, and no one could talk to him but his wife and one of his men under certain circumstances. Oral would stay in that room, praying to get the mind of God for the next meeting and waiting on the anointing. He once told me, "I *had* to feel the anointing before I went into the meeting to minister to the sick."

A restricted life is required to carry the anointings, impartations, and mantles of God, and you have to understand the cost.

Now, some folks can just get up and walk by faith to work in the anointing, but Brother Roberts was one who said, "I had to feel it. I wasn't leaving my room unless I felt God's power upon me." The tent meeting started at seven o'clock, and there would be 20,000-plus people in the tent. Thousands of sick people would be coming. Oral told me, "I couldn't face those people just being Oral Roberts, because nothing would happen!"

Oral refused to leave that room until he felt that mighty power upon him. Only then would he leave to enter the tent meeting, knowing he was ready to face the lost and dying and give them hope through the anointing of Almighty God. He would walk out on that stage — God's man of faith and power, Reverend Oral Roberts. Then *whoom!* — God's anointing would hit the room! And when he began to lay hands on people, they'd begin to get healed. Everyone present saw manifested before them visible evidence of the presence and the power of the Holy Spirit!

That's what we want!

The healing anointing that Oral had on him worked because of the restricted life he lived. He pulled himself away from what all others were doing, and he said, "This is the price required to have the healing anointing at the level of authority and manifestation I'm operating in."

Now, some people have a visitation or a one-time supernatural event in their lives, and they live off the memory of it forever. But what you want is a *life* of great acts of God, not just one act of God that defines your whole life.

Most Christians in the Western world pursue an event, not a life. But if God has called you to carry a mantle, you must get rid of the "event mentality" and come into a lifestyle of revival and anointing and of paying the price He requires.

"Brother Roberts, I can't do that." Then you can't have that. Now, you may be able to fake the anointing for a while, but when the real thing shows up, it will show *you* up — and everyone will recognize the difference.

What you want is a *life* of great acts of God, not just one act of God that defines your whole life.

THE COVENANTAL PRICE OF A MANTLE

As we've seen, the life that a person has to live to carry a mantle, or to carry certain key assignments in God, is a restricted life. Just because others can do certain things doesn't mean that the mantle carrier can.

The divine wooing of the Spirit to cause someone to accept the assignment of a mantle can sometimes result in an internal war. The person's flesh wants to say, *I have my own anointing! I don't want to just share the calling and anointing of those who have carried this mantle before me.*

But when someone inherits one of these mantles, it is obvious. When that person walks in a room and it's the real deal, everyone can see that the call and anointing is there.

There is the common price required of all who are believers, and then there is the unique covenantal price of the mantle carrier.

What is the common price? As believers, we are called to:

- Live holy lives.
- Build a strong foundation in God's Word.
- Manage our soul as we renew our mind with the Word.
- Cultivate an intimate prayer life with the Lord.
- Develop our spirit man so our natural reasoning doesn't dominate us and we become more conscious of God's indwelling presence than of the world around us.
- Continually "carry our cross," saying no to our own ways and surrendering to God's ways.

These are things we as Christians are all required to do.

Then for one called to inherit a mantle, the covenantal price sits on top of the common price. This involves the commitment this person must make with the Lord to work in that mantle.

The Lord will tell that person, *"To carry this mantle, these are requirements you must fulfill."* And for the one ordained to receive a mantle, there will be a time of consecration during which he or she covenants with the Lord: "What You say, I will do. I will pay the price. Even if You don't manifest Your power through me immediately, I will stay faithful."

God watches for a time to see if those called to inherit a mantle mean what they say. He watches to see if they have longevity with their commitment. He watches to see if they mourn their sacrifice. If they do mourn what they have given up, it wasn't a true sacrifice.

Now, if other people try to add that covenantal price to their lives when they're not called to do that, it's not going to work. For instance, some people try to take on the price that Kathryn Kuhlman paid to carry her healing mantle, but it goes nowhere because that isn't their calling. They will never be able to carry the price of a mantle that God never intended for them to carry.

**For one called to inherit a mantle,
the covenantal price sits on top of the common price.
This involves the commitment this person must make
with the Lord to work in that mantle.**

That's why it's so important for each of us to "stay in our lane" in the Body of Christ. We must diligently seek God first to know what He has specifically called *us* to do. Then we must continue seeking Him every day of our lives to know *how* He wants us to go about fulfilling that divine purpose while we are on this earth.

'IF YOU SEE ME...'

Look at what Elijah said next to the younger prophet: "So he said, 'You have asked a hard thing. Nevertheless, if you see me when I am taken from you, it shall be so for you; but if not, it shall not be *so.*'" (2 Kings 2:10 NKJV).

When the prophet Elijah was taken up to Heaven in the fiery chariot and horses, Elisha saw it — that was the requirement.

But beyond that, Elisha saw *Elijah*. He could have focused on the spectacular sight of the fiery chariot and horses and missed what he had so diligently pursued. If Elisha had become too enamored with and distracted by the spectacular, he would have lost the moment of the mantle transfer.

So there is a laser-focus requirement to the transfer of a mantle, and the successor must contend for that vital focus to the end.

As for Elisha, he kept his eyes on the prize, his focal point: *I must see him.* He was aware of the other, but it was not what his gaze was centered on. It would have been impossible to say the fiery chariot didn't get his attention, but Elisha knew he had to hold to the discipline of focus: *I have to keep my eyes on God and His purposes for my life, or I'm not going to receive what He has told me to pursue.*

There is a laser-focus requirement to the transfer of a mantle, and the successor must contend for that vital focus to the end.

I'll give you an example of how this principle can play out in the Church of our day. Sometimes potential successors become enamored by the public acclaim, the money, and the miracles God works through them. If they don't correct their focus, they are in danger of disqualifying themselves and missing what the Holy Spirit actually desired to accomplish through them. That is one of the reasons some mantles are not active in the earth today.

Often these called ones come from a background of relative poverty and obscurity, so they have to deal with challenges, both spiritually and emotionally, that arise from their lack of experience. For instance, preachers can struggle with emotional feelings about money. When spiritual principles of obedience and sowing into the Kingdom are activated, they begin to increase financially.

But for preachers who haven't grown up with much money, their emotions in the financial realm may still be that of an adolescent. They've never before had substantial funds to steward; before this, they have lived a life of just trying to make it. So if money starts flowing in, these ministers may make the mistake of getting their focus on the money rather than on God and His purposes.

If that happens, these ministers can make mistakes regarding how they handle the ministry funds. It eventually becomes evident that they don't have the emotional maturity or natural wisdom necessary to make wise financial decisions that protect their God-given assignment.

Then there is the minister's challenge not to focus on the popularity and the public acclaim. Fame is one of the most powerful commodities a minister can have to promote the Gospel — but it can also kill that minister in a New York minute!

If fame becomes a part of your identity, you are in trouble. It's right to seek the Holy Spirit's wisdom on how to use any public acclaim you have gained as a commodity to promote the Lord's work and further His Kingdom. But fame is *not* something you are, and it is not to be used to your own selfish advantage.

So this principle found in Elijah's words to Elisha is critically important. To those called to receive a mantle, the Lord asks: *"What are you focusing on?"* No matter what might try to distract, the answer must be Christ only and the high mark of His calling (*see* Heb. 12:2; Phil. 3:14).

'THE CHANGING OF THE GUARD'

The passing of a mantle represents a generational shift. One era is ending, and a new one is beginning with a changing of the guard.

That spiritual reality was demonstrated when Elisha ripped his clothes in two after Elijah was suddenly translated to Heaven in a fiery chariot and horses. The rending of one's clothes was a Jewish gesture of honor and intense emotion at the departing of one who was beloved. But I believe Elisha's rending of his clothes was also symbolic of removing the old to make way for the new mantle that was coming.

**The passing of a mantle represents
a generational shift. One era is ending,
and a new one is beginning
with a changing of the guard.**

Elisha was getting ready to receive the fulfillment of his long pursuit. All that he had known up to that moment in his life would bow to the weighty mantle assignment he was about to pick up. All that Elisha had been learning by serving and walking with Elijah was about to become part of the younger prophet's new function.

It was time for Elisha to lay aside his former life and embrace the new. There was a new generation to reach as God's prophetic mouthpiece. A mantle had been discarded and left for Elisha to pick up and carry forward. And the moment the prophet struck the water with that mantle and walked forward on dry land, a new phase of the divine plan began in the power of the double anointing.

Chapter 7

Qualified to Ask

What gave Elisha the right to ask for a double portion of Elijah's mantle? Let's take some time answering that question, because we need to better understand what it means to qualify for such a weighty gift from Heaven.

For one thing, Elisha had been consistent in ministering to Elijah as his disciple, his servant, and his spiritual son. God had placed that prophetic call on Elisha's life; others had observed that call; and he had diligently pursued the preparation that was necessary to become qualified.

Elisha's consistent faithfulness to follow Elijah closely and to serve him unconditionally earned the younger man the right to request that double portion when it came time to transfer the mantle. Through the years, others visited Elijah, but only Elisha had lived with him and ministered to him. The association factor was very healthy and strong in his relationship to the elder prophet.

We know by biblical record that God was faithful to supply what Elisha asked for. The double portion was in manifestation during the years of Elisha's ministry, with Elisha ultimately performing twice as many miracles as Elijah did. (*See* "Elisha's Double-Portion Anointing Manifested" below; text continues to page 102.)

**Elisha's consistent faithfulness
to follow Elijah closely and to serve him unconditionally
earned the younger man the right to request
that double portion when it came time
to transfer the mantle.**

ELISHA'S DOUBLE-PORTION ANOINTING MANIFESTED

Miracles in the Career of Elijah

1. Causing the rain the cease for 3½ years (1 Kings 17:1).
2. Being fed by the ravens (1 Kings 17:4).
3. Miracle of the barrel of meal and cruse of oil (1 Kings 17:14).
4. Resurrection of the widow's son (1 Kings 17:22).
5. Calling of fire from Heaven on the altar (1 Kings 18:38).
6. Causing it to rain (1 Kings 18:45).
7. Prophecy that Ahab's sons would all be destroyed (1 Kings 21:22).
8. Prophecy that Jezebel would be eaten by dogs (1 Kings 21:23).

9. Prophecy that Ahaziah would die of his illness (2 Kings 1:4).

10. Calling fire from Heaven upon the first 50 soldiers (2 Kings 1:10).

11. Calling fire from Heaven upon the second 50 soldiers (2 Kings 1:12).

12. Parting of the Jordan (2 Kings 2:8).

13. Prophecy that Elisha should have a double portion of his spirit (2 Kings 2:10).

14. Being caught up to Heaven in a whirlwind (2 Kings 2:11).

Miracles in the Career of Elisha

1. Parting of the Jordan (2 Kings 2:14).

2. Healing of the waters (2 Kings 2:21).

3. Curse of the she bears (2 Kings 2:24).

4. Filling of the valley with water (2 Kings 3:17).

5. Deception of the Moabites with the valley of blood (2 Kings 3:22).

6. Miracle of the vessels of oil (2 Kings 4:4).

7. Prophecy that the Shunammite woman would have a son (2 Kings 4:16).

8. Resurrection of the Shunammite's son (2 Kings 4:34).

9. Healing of the gourds (2 Kings 4:41).

10. Miracle of the bread (2 Kings 4:43).

11. Healing of Naaman (2 Kings 5:14).

12. Perception of Gehazi's transgression (2 Kings 5:26).

13. Cursing Gehazi with leprosy (2 Kings 5:27).

14. Floating of the axe-head (2 Kings 6:6).

15. Prophecy of the Syrian battle plans (2 Kings 6:9).

16. Vision of the chariots (2 Kings 6:17).

17. Smiting the Syrian army with blindness (2 Kings 6:18).

18. Restoring the sight of the Syrian army (2 Kings 6:20).

19. Prophecy of the end of the great famine (2 Kings 7:1).

20. Prophecy that the scoffing nobleman would see, but not partake of, the abundance (2 Kings 7:2).

21. Deception of the Syrians with the sound of chariots (2 Kings 7:6).

22. Prophecy of the seven-year famine (2 Kings 8:1).

23. Prophecy of Benhadad's untimely death (2 Kings 8:10).

24. Prophecy of Hazael's cruelty to Israel (2 Kings 8:12).

25. Prophecy that Jehu would smite the house of Ahab (2 Kings 9:7).

26. Prophecy that Joash would smite the Syrians at Aphek (2 Kings 13:17).

27. Prophecy that Joash would smite Syria three times but not consume it (2 Kings 13:19).

28. Resurrection of the man touched by Elisha's bones (2 Kings 13:21).

No Advertising Needed

As mentioned earlier, a mantle is transferred primarily through three factors: *close association*, *environment*, and *influence through pursuit*. That is why the successor will sometimes show traits of the one who came before — which is entirely different than someone imitating a person in the natural.

This only in part helps explain why a mantle is recognizable. The greater reality is the divine transfer that has taken place in the Spirit. Once the successor has inherited the mantle, he doesn't have to announce it. It will be evident without any advertising.

> **And when the sons of the prophets which were to view at Jericho saw him, they said, The spirit of Elijah doth rest on Elisha. And they came to meet him, and bowed themselves to the ground before him.**
>
> **2 Kings 2:15**

The sons of the prophet recognized what had happened. They were spiritually tuned to a degree, so they knew. They didn't have to surmise it.

In other words, the sons of the prophets accepted Elisha as the one who had inherited the office and anointing of Elijah, and they bowed down in acknowledgment and said, "So be it." They saw Elisha operating in the office he had inherited; yet Elisha never said to them or anyone else, "I am the successor to Elijah's ministry."

So we see that when a person has received a mantle, no convincing is required. He or she simply walks in the spiritual equipment of the mantle and allows God to demonstrate Himself. People will know. That's the way it works.

But before that happens, the price must be paid, and that's largely why it takes time. Especially concerning these top mantles that often carry governmental influence, the ministers who have carried them in times past operated in God's mighty power and strength. There is a great deal that God has to trust the successor with before He turns up that power.

For instance, Kathryn Kuhlman didn't begin to operate in miracles until the last 25 years or so of her life because she had to rework and rebuild her life and ministry after making a great error of judgment in marriage (*see* Chapter 16). Afterward, she and God had to get back into covenant, and eventually she began doing very well in her region. The miracles began to multiply, and the crowds began coming in greater and greater numbers.

The other factor that greatly accelerated Kathryn's ministry was the inception of her media ministry on radio and television. This gave her a natural platform that put her before millions of people.

When a person has received a mantle, no convincing is required. He or she simply walks in the spiritual equipment of the mantle and allows God to demonstrate Himself.

However, it's important to understand the sequence of events in the life of Kathryn Kuhlman. First, she paid the price; then God began providing open doors of opportunity that put her before the people.

That's also how Oral Roberts and Billy Graham became famous. When they added a media platform to their ministry, they were brought before the consciousness of the people. They weren't trying to build their ego; their hearts were to reach more people. And the Lord used that platform to push them into the public's awareness.

Kenneth E. Hagin also went for years in the ministry with only a relatively few listening to him. But then through his books, his radio program, and his widening reach into denominational circles during the growing Charismatic Movement of the 1960s, Brother Hagin began to gain a national voice, and everything shifted in his ministry.

There is normally this media component that develops for these top mantles that enlarges their voice over the voice of the enemy.

We first see this concept in the account of Hannah, the prophet Samuel's mother, as she prophesied after the birth of this child she had so fervently prayed for. Hannah used this phrase: "...My mouth is enlarged over mine enemies..." (1 Sam. 2:1).

What happens is this: There comes a moment in the spiritual journey of mantle carriers when the voice of God through *their* voice overtakes the voice of the enemy. It is the weight of divine authority they carry and speak from that begins to attract the masses and exponentially increase their popularity. God turns up the power when He knows He can trust them to faithfully carry the weight of His glory demonstrated and the fame of man that will inevitably follow.

THOSE WHO 'VIEW AFAR OFF'

I've just described the powerful mark of a mantle carrier that is evident to all when in demonstration.

In contrast, we can look again at the sons of the prophets mentioned in 2 Kings 2:15: "...The sons of the prophets which were to view at Jericho saw him, they said, The spirit of Elijah doth rest on Elisha. And they came to meet him and bowed themselves to the ground before him."

**There comes a moment in the spiritual journey
of mantle carriers when the voice of God
through *their* voice overtakes
the voice of the enemy.**

As I mentioned earlier, the sons of the prophets were those who settled for the distant view in the crucial hours leading up to his departure. Once Elisha received Elijah's mantle and parted the Jordan River with it, the sons of the prophets came and bowed before Elisha in a sign of submission and in acknowledgment of him as the inheritor of Elijah's mantle. In that act, they were saying, "I recognize this; I accept this; and I will follow the prophet Elisha as I followed Elijah."

To me, this also reveals something else about the sons of the prophets. They were the kind of folks who could have been something more but likely never would be. They were in the prophetic camp; they saw and heard things beyond the natural realm. But they never took the initiative to pay the price required to obtain the ultimate prize.

The sons of the prophets just knew the headline: Elijah would depart soon. But they didn't position themselves to stay close to the prophet or to understand more concerning what was about to transpire. Instead, they "…went and stood to view afar off" (2 Kings 2:7).

**The sons of the prophets just knew the headline:
Elijah would depart soon.
But they didn't position themselves
to stay close to the prophet
or to understand more concerning
what was about to transpire.**

It is important to note that after Elijah had gone to Heaven, the sons of the prophets came to a faulty conclusion from their distant viewpoint. They knew about the prophet's departure, but they thought he might have fallen off the chariot!

And they said unto him, Behold now, there be with thy servants fifty strong men; let them go, we pray thee, and seek thy master: lest peradventure the Spirit of the Lord hath taken him up, and cast him upon some mountain, or into some valley. And he said, Ye shall not send. And when they urged him till he was ashamed, he said, Send. They sent therefore fifty men; and they sought three days, but found him not. And when they came again to him, (for he tarried at Jericho,) he said unto them, Did I not say unto you, Go not?

2 Kings 2:16-18

The sons of the prophets kept urging Elisha to let them go look for the body of the prophet until he was embarrassed to refuse them. Elisha finally gave in and told them to go ahead and look, sending 50 members of the group on a quest that he knew was futile. For three days, they looked, and, of course, they found nothing.

In my view, that reveals the lack of spiritual intelligence that these sons of the prophets possessed. They could know some things in the spiritual realm, but they didn't know how to process what they knew in order to come to right conclusions. Perhaps that is why they were called "the sons" and not "the prophets." They had a little ability to discern, but not enough for people to follow them.

As if God were going to let the prophet He had worked with for years drop off the fiery chariot! As if He were going to leave Elijah's dead body somewhere on some mountain so that the sons of the prophets would have to go find and bury his body!

Some parts of the Body of Christ even today are full of "sons of the prophets" rather than true, seasoned prophets of God. They are out in the world acting foolishly, trying to receive a prophetic anointing that they're not ready for. They know and can see some things, and some of what they say may be true. But they often don't come to right conclusions, and as a result, they participate in unwise ventures mislabeled "spiritual" that fit in the category of "Let's go hunt for Elijah's body"!

People who fit in this category have failed to maintain a healthy, common-sense life, grounded in the strength of the Word. And sometimes as you talk with such people, you might have a thought, *You believe such silliness, and you want me to follow you? No. I may have dinner with you, but I'll not follow you.*

As for the prophet Elijah, he was indeed gone; the sons of the prophets had gotten that much right. But his body wasn't out there lying on some hill, having fallen off the chariot! Yet that's what some of them were saying.

That's why the sons of the prophets were still in prophet school! Maybe they would have to be in school for the rest of their lives. Regardless, in this case, only one was actually qualified to receive the prophet's mantle — the one who had paid the price to stay close and learn well how to hear what God was saying and operate in His power effectively according to His instruction.

As for the prophet Elijah, he was indeed gone; the sons of the prophets had gotten that much right. But his body wasn't out there lying on some hill, having fallen off the chariot. Yet that's what some of them were saying.

That's why the sons of the prophets were still in-prophet school. Maybe they would have to be in school for the rest of their lives. Regardless, in this case only one was actually qualified to receive the prophet's mantle — the one who had paid the price to stay close and learn well how to hear what God was saying and operate in His power effectively according to His instruction.

Chapter 8

THE COST OF SAYING YES

Elisha performed his first miracle at the Jordan River, parting the water with the prophet's mantle he had inherited. Afterward, Elisha had been standing in his office as Elijah's successor for only a short time when he was faced with his first experience with persecution.

In Elisha's journey afterward to Bethel, he encountered some mocking "youths" (in Jewish culture, most likely referring to a group of young men in their 20s). These arrogant young men made fun of Elisha's appearance by calling him a "baldhead."

> Then he went up from there to Bethel; and as he was going up the road, some youths came from the city and mocked him, and said to him, "Go up, you baldhead! Go up, you baldhead!" So he turned around and looked at them, and pronounced a curse on them in the name of the Lord. And two female bears came out of the woods and mauled forty-two of the youths. Then he went from there to Mount Carmel, and from there he returned to Samaria.
>
> **2 Kings 2:23-25 NKJV**

We don't know much else about Elisha's appearance, other than that he was bald. But we know that these arrogant young men opened a door to the enemy with their act of mocking God's prophet that resulted in their destruction.

Persecution and opposition accompanies any significant act of obedience to the Lord. That certainly includes the act of saying *yes* to the responsibility of assuming a mantle.

Righteous persecution actually occurs *because* a man or woman of God is doing right and preaching right. That means the obedient one has a responsibility not to pull back from obeying God, no matter what opposition comes his or her way. Jesus Himself said one of the consequences of living for Him in this fallen world is to be persecuted because of righteousness' sake (*see* Matt. 5:10; Mark 10:29-30).

With that in mind, it's interesting to note that Elisha had barely gotten out of the gate as Elijah's successor before opposition from strange places showed up to stop his progress.

**Persecution and opposition accompanies
any significant act of obedience to the Lord.
That certainly includes the act
of saying *yes* to the responsibility
of assuming a mantle.**

There are two kinds of righteous persecution against God's people:

1. Persecution because of ignorance. People act to oppose the truth, but they don't know that what they're doing is wrong because they are ignorant. When they learn the truth, they begin to do right, which stops the persecution.

2. Self-induced persecution — when people know better, but they go ahead and persecute the righteous anyway. In that case, it's the persecutors' fault. They can't even blame the devil for the consequences they suffer for persecuting the righteous. They created their own mess.

This second kind of persecution was the case with the group of mockers who harassed the prophet Elisha as he made his way to Bethel. The young men were the makers of their own destruction by yielding to the enemy's attempt to scorn and belittle the holy transaction that had just taken place at the Jordan River.

THE RESPONSIBILITY TO COMPLETE UNFINISHED BUSINESS

There is another key part of the price to pay to qualify as the successor of a mantle. He or she must be willing to complete or to correct any unfinished business left by the one who came before. We can see this principle play out in the lives of Elijah and Elisha.

After Elijah's great victory when pitted against Jezebel's 400 prophets of Baal on Mount Carmel, he faced the backlash of the queen's fury. Elijah ran from Jezebel's wrath, traveling many miles before stopping to rest in a cave on Mount Horeb. It was there that God visited him and gave him three assignments:

And the Lord said unto him, Go, return on thy way to the wilderness of Damascus: and when thou comest, anoint Hazael to be king over Syria: And Jehu the son of Nimshi shalt thou anoint to be king over Israel: and Elisha the son of Shaphat of Abelmeholah shalt thou anoint to be prophet in thy room. And it shall come to pass, that him that escapeth the sword of Hazael shall Jehu slay: and him that escapeth from the sword of Jehu shall Elisha slay.

1 Kings 19:15-17

God told the prophet Elijah to: 1) anoint Hazael as king of Syria; 2) anoint Jehu as king of Israel; and 3) anoint Elisha as prophet in his place, bringing him under his tutorship. But of those three instructions, the Bible only records that Elijah accomplished one of them before being translated to Heaven. After his encounter with the Lord on Mount Horeb, Elijah traveled to where Elisha lived and put him in place to be trained as the prophet who would succeed him (*see* vv. 19-21).

I want to offer two different views from well-respected theologians for consideration. Both address the lack of any scriptural record stating that Elijah himself fulfilled two of the three divine directives that he was given by the Lord.

First, let's look at the 18th-century theologian Albert Barnes' approach to these three governmental tasks that God gave Elijah. Barnes viewed the way these tasks were ultimately fulfilled through the lens of divine timing and strategic ordering of events.

Elijah performed one only of the three commissions given to him. He appears to have been left free to choose the time for executing his commissions, and it would seem that he thought the proper occasion had not arisen either for the first or the second before his own translation. But he took care to communicate the divine commands to his successor, who performed them at the fitting moment.[4]

The 19th-century theologian James Burton Coffman had a different view on this subject. Coffman contended that a lack of scriptural record doesn't necessarily mean that Elijah didn't fulfill all of the divine instructions himself.

> The three things that God commanded Elijah to do are nowhere stated in the O.T. as having been done by Elijah, but this is no problem. We may be certain that Elijah indeed obeyed the heavenly commandments, even if our extremely abbreviated records do not tell us anything about how or when he did so. Furthermore, the fact of some other person being cited as anointing Jehu at a later time is probably another anointing.[5]

I tend to agree with Albert Barnes' position, but with a few added thoughts. I believe that Elisha, after assuming Elijah's position as foremost prophet in the land, was charged with the responsibility of ensuring that these two governmental tasks were carried out in the right timing for God's prophetic words to be fulfilled. Elisha was to finish what Elijah had been assigned to do.

However, I also believe it's possible that Elijah was taken early because he didn't fulfill those two assignments God gave him on Mount Horeb. I understand that this isn't something we can know for certain one way or the other until we get to Heaven. But something I've observed over the years in studying the lives of God's prophets may pertain here: If they didn't act on certain things that the Lord instructed them to do prophetically, many times they left the earth early.

[4] Albert Barnes, *Barnes' Notes on the Old and New Testament*, 1 Kings 19:15-17, Public Domain.
[5] James Burton Coffman, *Coffman's Commentaries on the Bible, 1 Kings* (Abilene, TX: Abilene Christian University Press, May 1974.)

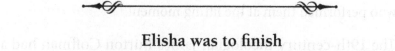

Elisha was to finish
what Elijah had been assigned to do.

After Elijah's great victory on Mt. Carmel with the prophets of Baal, Jezebel's intimidation caused him to run many miles until he reached a cave on Mt. Horeb. There the Lord asked the prophet, "What are you doing here, Elijah?"

It's evident that Elijah was inwardly struggling as he sat inside that cave. His response to the Lord not only wasn't correct, but it also came from a somewhat selfish and even prideful state of discouragement: "...I have been very zealous for the Lord God of hosts; because the children of Israel have forsaken Your covenant, torn down Your altars, and killed Your prophets with the sword. I alone am left; and they seek to take my life" (1 Kings 19:14 NKJV).

Elijah had taken a hit when Jezebel threatened him and responded in the flesh. But later God set Elijah back in place with His answer to Elijah's despair that he was the only faithful one left: "I have 7,000 who still serve Me" (*see* v. 18).

It was in the context of correcting Elijah's misperception that the Lord gave him those three governmental tasks to complete — and, as far as we know, Elijah completed only one. Yet Elijah still had several years left on earth as Israel's number-one prophet. During those years, he would train Elisha as successor to the mantle, and he did that well. We can also safely assume that he had a role in training the sons of the prophets who are mentioned.

Three of the eight miracles recorded during Elijah's ministry would take place in the latter part of those final years (*see* 2 Kings 2:8,10,11). But as far as we can know from the record of Scripture, Elijah would not be the one to complete two of the three governmental tasks given to him by the Lord during his last years on earth.

So included in the price of receiving Elijah's mantle was Elisha's responsibility to complete any unfinished business of this one who came before.

God never wants a continuation of missteps in the next generation. If different factors cause a delay in accomplishing certain assigned tasks in one generation, He will be looking for those mantle responsibilities to be completed in the next.

Elisha fulfilled Elijah's two unfinished governmental tasks during his tenure of that mantle assignment (*see* 2 Kings 8:7-15; 9:1-10). It's possible that Elijah delegated these tasks to Elisha as the successor to be done at a later time. It's also possible that those assigned tasks simply should have been done during Elijah's time.

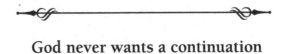

God never wants a continuation of missteps in the next generation.

Regardless, it seems that a part of Elisha's responsibilities in carrying the prophet's mantle was to take care of his predecessor's unfinished business according to God's instructions. And Elisha was diligent to ensure that this responsibility was fulfilled.

That quality of diligence defined Elisha's ministry from the moment he picked up Elijah's mantle. Scripture reveals that Elisha was faithful to fulfill his assignment throughout his life, walking in that double portion of anointing to accomplish God's will in his generation.

Chapter 9

SPIRITUAL FATHERS AND SONS

L et's backtrack a bit to that amazing, significant moment when Elisha saw Elijah taken away in a fiery chariot. I want us to focus in on the relationship that was forged between the elder and the younger man in the years they walked together.

> **And it came to pass, as they still went on, and talked, that, behold, there appeared a chariot of fire, and horses of fire, and parted them both asunder; and Elijah went up by a whirlwind into heaven. And Elisha saw it, and he cried, My father, my father, the chariot of Israel, and the horsemen thereof. And he saw him no more: and he took hold of his own clothes, and rent them in two pieces.**
>
> **2 Kings 2:11-12**

Notice the words Elisha uttered as he beheld that heavenly sight. He did *not* cry out, "My mentor, my mentor!" or, "My life coach, my life coach!" Elisha spontaneously cried out, "My father, my father!"

I appreciate the value of the mentor and life-coach roles. They have a place in life — but it's not this place. Fathering in the Spirit, or being a mother in the Spirit, is what one called to inherit a mantle needs more than a mentor or a life coach. Spiritual parenting is actually something every believer needs.

LIFE COACH VS. SPIRITUAL PARENTING

Sometimes people engage the services of a life coach to help them navigate life successfully, and they begin to think that this person is their spiritual parent. But a life coach fills a different role in a person's life.

People need more than a life coach. They need a guiding influence who is stronger and deeper in their lives than a mentor. People need a spiritual parent.

In fact, I believe the key to the successful transfer of a mantle is in the parenting of the elder and the sonship of the one who is called to inherit the divine assignment. The parent teaches the son (or daughter) the ways of Christian living and how to work with that mantle.

One who is a parent to you has a deeper relationship with you than you would have with a mentor or a life coach. We use those terms today, and it's true that mentorship and life coaching is encompassed in parenting. But parenting is not that alone.

Sometimes what we really need is someone who will correct us — someone who will get in our face and tell us the way things are. A mom and a dad just have a way of telling us the facts of life.

A life coach or a mentor might suggest the truth of a situation and hope that you get it. But when a mom or a dad talks to you, you're going to get the truth, whether you like it or not! Mentors and life coaches don't want to get that "sticky" in the nitty gritty of your life — but mom and dad will.

**People need more than a life coach.
They need a guiding influence who is stronger
and deeper in their lives than a mentor.
People need a spiritual parent.**

So the way Elisha spontaneously cried out, "My father!" when Elijah suddenly was taken away speaks volumes. It tells us that Elijah had crossed over that line in Elisha's life into the working with the secret character, thoughts, and fears of the private person. That's what a parent does, and it's what a life coach or a mentor cannot or would not do.

THE VALUE OF DISCOVERING
A SPIRITUAL FATHER

This relationship between a spiritual father and son is pivotal in preparing for the transfer of a mantle. But it's important to note here that although I am focusing primarily on the father-son relationship, the principles absolutely apply to spiritual mothers and daughters as well. We need mamas of Zion and mothers of Israel as much as we need fathers of the faith to ensure a successful transition of mantles from generation to generation.

There are normally three kinds of father relationships that believers are to nurture in their lives: First is their Heavenly Father; second is their natural father; and third is their spiritual father. (I should note that for some people, their natural father could fill the role of their spiritual father as well, depending on the father's spiritual maturity and the closeness of the relationship.) This is especially true with those called to inherit a mantle.

Spiritual fathers are rare to come by, but they do exist, and it's crucial that we recognize the nature and the value of that person or persons when they fill that role in our lives. And one truth we have to learn right up front is this: We don't choose our spiritual father — we *discover* him.

As Christians, we are all seeking to walk the path God planned out for us before the foundations of the earth (*see* Eph. 2:10). That path includes the church body we are to become a part of and the people we are to be closely connected with.

We are not drawn together just out of convenience. God places; God plants; and God establishes. When we are serving the Lord with all our hearts and seeking to be led by the Spirit, none of our godly close associations are by accident, for God is the One who orchestrates.

For a potential successor to a mantle, this reality certainly includes his spiritual father. It is the younger one's responsibility to discover who his father is and then to learn from him. It will be the father's heart to watch over the soul of his spiritual son and train him in the ways of God.

One truth we have to learn right up front is this:
We don't choose our spiritual father —
we *discover* him.

The Apostle Paul talked to the church at Corinth about this spiritual truth in 1 Corinthians 4:15:

For though ye have ten thousand instructors in Christ, yet have ye not many fathers: for in Christ Jesus, I have begotten you through the gospel.

Notice that Paul differentiated between two different roles in the believers' lives. He was saying to the believers in that church, "You have many instructors — people who can teach the Bible to you and bless you with their scriptural knowledge — but you don't have many spiritual parents. I am your spiritual dad; I'm not just an instructor to you. There is a difference."

This is so important to understand, because so many people in the world today are looking for covering, and rightfully so. We need a proper covering of protection, blessing, and guidance from a spiritual father or mother who thrills in our success.

But sometimes believers submit themselves to an elder brother or sister, and that order of relationship doesn't work long term.

Other times people submit to what I call slave masters. These individuals may hold a position of authority in people's lives, but they are there for the people's names, phone numbers, addresses, attendance, and money. There is no cultivated relationship. In fact, these leaders seldom have much personal interaction with the people at all.

**So many people in the world today
are looking for covering, and rightfully so.
We need a proper covering of protection, blessing,
and guidance from a spiritual father or mother
who thrills in our success.**

Leaders who fit in this "slave master" category build their own fleshly form of authority structure and then accuse the son of being rebellious if he won't conform. That is not a spiritual parent. That is a user and an abuser — a slave master who is milking the son for everything he's got, and the son is going to wake up one morning with nothing.

Those in training to receive a mantle should avoid entering into that kind of relationship at all cost. They need to be part of a true spiritual covering and know who their spiritual father is.

We can see the biblical pattern of a spiritual mother in the life of Deborah. In Judges 5:7 when Deborah came to power over the people of Israel, she said, "...I arose as a mother in Israel." Deborah didn't come as a queen; she didn't come as a princess; she didn't come with vengeance or rage. Deborah came as a *mother* — and when Mama comes to power, that nation gets turned around!

That's one of the great things about a spiritual parent. Deborah came as a mother and helped the people of Israel get back on their feet the way they should go.

So we want Deborahs; we want Abrahams. We want spiritual fathers and mothers in our lives.

AN INSTRUCTOR VS. A FATHER

Notice again what the Apostle Paul was saying in 1 Corinthians 4:15. He said there are many instructors but very few spiritual parents. Paul wasn't saying that instructors are wrong or bad; he was just saying that they are not parents. He was making the point to the Corinthian congregation, "I am your spiritual father; I have begotten you in the gospel of Jesus Christ." This was important for the Corinthian believers to understand, because they had some big problems that Paul had to confront and deal with.

That church was experiencing exciting services with many manifestations of the gifts of the Spirit; however, they couldn't keep their morality right. For one thing, they were celebrating the Lord's Supper by feasting and getting drunk. So as the spiritual father of that church, Paul was "spanking their behinds," telling them what they had to do to put things back in order (*see* 1 Cor. 11:20-34).

When Paul was saying, "You have many instructors in Christ," he was talking about those people we have in our lives who are called and gifted to instruct us in some capacity in our spiritual walk. Paul meant no disregard toward those he called instructors in Christ. He wasn't trying to diminish their role in our lives; he was simply highlighting the difference between their role and a spiritual father's role.

Misconceptions About Spiritual Parents

Let me share a few points on what a spiritual parent is *not* to make it easier for you to recognize the role of a true spiritual parent in another person's life or in your own life.

1st Misconception

A spiritual parent is usually not the one who got you saved. Now, sometimes that can be true, but it is usually not the case.

The person who led you to the Lord will always deserve honor and hold a special place in your heart and life for being the soulwinner who helped bring you into the Kingdom. But that person is not automatically your spiritual parent.

2nd Misconception

A person whose teachings have really blessed you and helped you out in your walk with God does not automatically become your spiritual parent. That person is most likely your instructor in Christ. Please receive the impartation he or she is making available to you, but know the difference between a spiritual parent and an instructor.

I was talking with a couple one day, and they told me, "Our spiritual mom is Joyce Meyer."

I replied, "Oh, great, how is she doing?"

They replied, "Well, we assume she's doing good."

"You don't know? Didn't you say that you were her spiritual children? Doesn't that mean you have a relationship of some kind with Joyce Meyer?"

"Oh, no, we just watch Joyce on television; her teaching blesses us."

Now, that actually describes an instructor's role in a person's life. That is not a spiritual parent.

We often get the roles all mixed up that people are to fill in our lives. We may call certain individuals our spiritual parents who actually fill the role of mentor, life coach, or instructor. Yet what we really need watching over our lives are those who are caring and mature enough to be true spiritual parents.

So many times we love the ministers who bring blessing and impartation into our lives as we sit under their teaching, and we call them our fathers and mothers in the faith. And certainly the impact and the influence of these men and women of God is tremendous, because some of them occupy the position as fathers and mothers of the Church at large.

We may call certain individuals our spiritual parents who actually fill the role of mentor, life coach, or instructor. Yet what we really need watching over our lives are those who are caring and mature enough to be true spiritual parents.

But the ones to whom we often don't give the respect we should are those we can call our personal spiritual fathers and mothers. These are the precious people in our lives who "changed our diapers" spiritually — the ones who walked down the road with us and helped us recover from the times we took a wrong turn or stumbled along the way.

3rd Misconception

Having a person in your life who always agrees with you does not mean you have found your spiritual parent. In fact, it actually means you have someone in your life you can't trust as your primary counsel because that person is going to say only what you want him to say.

Someone might say, "But this person just loves my ministry. He understands me and supports me." Great! But does he have the right to correct you or to tell you no? That's part of being a spiritual parent.

If you know that person's input will always be positive, you must realize that this doesn't describe the revelational or instructional counseling that needs to come with spiritual parenting. You may enjoy doing things together in ministry and life. That person may be your friend and someone you can talk to. But what he or she says to you won't carry the weight of accountability and in-depth commitment that the words of a spiritual parent must carry with you.

A parent has to be able to say, "Yes, that's good," or "No, stop that; you need to do this instead."

4th Misconception

A spiritual parent is not one with whom the son or daughter has a casual relationship with no accountability. Spiritual parenting requires more commitment. Spiritual parents have to be willing get their hands dirty — to possibly wear the mud of their spiritual children's mistakes upon their own reputation and ministry.

Yes, you can have a close friendship with your spiritual parent, but you must also have interaction that demands accountability. Most relationships that people call their spiritual covering do not have this kind of accountability.

Whom the Lord loves, He corrects (*see* Prov. 3:12). The same is true with a spiritual parent. The one who loves his spiritual children will correct them.

At first you may feel a little offended when a spiritual father asks questions about your private life. You may be tempted to ask, "Who do you think you are?"

But if you did ask that, a spiritual father would simply answer, "I am Dad, and I want to know the people you've been running with."

Whom the Lord loves, He corrects.
The same is true with a spiritual parent.
The one who loves his spiritual children
will correct them.

You may say, "Well, I don't want this kind of relationship." Then you don't want accountability.

And I've learned this principle over the years: Spiritual parents discover their spiritual children only after the second correction. How spiritual sons and daughters respond to correction is a sign of their submission to that parenting relationship God has appointed for them. The first correction may be met with acceptance. But it's the second correction when the realization hits: *Oh, this kind of thing is going to happen more often than just once!*

That's when the spiritual parent discovers: Will this person truly be a spiritual son? Or will he run off to find someone to tickle his ears and make him feel good, giving him what he wants to hear instead of what he needs to hear?

How spiritual sons and daughters respond to correction is a sign of their submission to that parenting relationship God has appointed for them.

If you live right, you have nothing to hide. If you're sincere of heart, you have nothing within you that resists a correction or an admonishment to be careful. An encouraging statement will not inflate your ego; it will encourage your soul to continue down the road you're currently traveling.

A TRUE SPIRITUAL FATHER

Write this down: There are no perfect fathers or perfect mothers, but there can be better hearts, sincere hearts, good hearts.

A true father can also say, "I was wrong," whereas a counterfeit father will not. Instead, he'll try to spiritualize the situation to offload the blame on someone else. But a true father or mother will say, "You know, I thought I was right, but since then I've learned I was wrong, and I'm sorry."

That builds something inside the relationship. It reveals one who is more concerned with character and integrity issues than with their gifting. Now, that doesn't mean a spiritual parent isn't going to deal with the giftings and anointing of their spiritual children. But they will deal with character first and with a stronger focus.

Why is this? Because whereas a gift is *given*, a person's character has to be *constructed*. The foundation has to be laid correctly. The beams have to be placed accurately. The connections have to be screwed in just right. To build a strong edifice of strong, godly character on the inside of a person takes time. Nowhere is this principle truer or more critical than in the preparation time of one who is in training to receive a mantle.

Let's talk about what spiritual parenting is actually supposed to look like. Keep in mind throughout our discussion that this was the relationship that Elijah cultivated with Elisha during the years that the younger served the elder. It was all according to God's plan and in preparation for the day when the prophetic mantle would be transferred to the next generation.

#1: An Extension of the Father's Heart

It's important to understand that spiritual parenting isn't something that man has created to control and manipulate our lives. It is a concept that comes down from Heaven to earth, from the Father's heart to ours, because He wants to have someone in the natural in our lives who is closely walking with Him and whom He can use to help us. This realization helps us accept the responsibility of participating in the relationship in order to receive its benefits.

#2: Raises Children from Immaturity to Proper Growth and Order

Many Christians are never truly parented spiritually, and sometimes their lack of training can be seen in how they behave.

Just having a child and letting him run wild is not parenting. Anyone can produce a baby. It takes someone with discipline and commitment to raise a child.

The same principle is true in the things of the Spirit. A spiritual parent is one who helps bring spiritual children out of immaturity into divine order. The goal is to help the spiritual son or daughter understand God's ways: what proper conduct looks like and what it means to walk in spiritual maturity. That means a spiritual parent has to be someone who is willing to confront even the uncomfortable or embarrassing traits and actions of the spiritual son or daughter.

A spiritual parent is one who helps bring spiritual children out of immaturity into divine order.

If a person isn't willing to confront the immaturities, the disrespectful moments, and the "out of orders" that sometimes arise in the life of the son, that person cannot stand in the position of a spiritual father. And if a son is submitting to someone who won't confront him or deal with him when he needs to be corrected, that son is submitted to someone who isn't a true spiritual father.

#3: Focuses More on Character Than Gifting

As I mentioned earlier, a true spiritual father is one who is more focused on dealing with your character than your gifting. Gifting is not first in a spiritual father's thinking as he trains.

A gifting does need support and understanding, but not at the expense of character. The gifts God gives His people that operate in their lives sit first on the foundation of character. If there is no foundation of character, the gift will eventually veer off track, blow up, or disappear.

Character can be explained many different ways, but a comment made by the great evangelist, D. L. Moody, has stuck with me: "Character is what you are in the dark." In essence, Moody was saying that character is what we are when no one is watching.

So when a spiritual father assists in building a son's character, he helps guarantee a stable life for that son. The father knows that when a son's character is built strong, that son's integrity will preserve him and he will be guaranteed longevity of success in both his spiritual and natural life.

#4: Speaks Words That Cause Needed Change

A true spiritual parent is one whose words have the ability to go beyond the surface of your soul right down into your inner person, to the core of who you really are. He can speak to you with such power that his words cause needed realignment and adjustment.

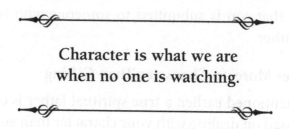

Character is what we are when no one is watching.

#5: Gives Sonship and an Inheritance

A true spiritual father is one who rescues spiritual children from the doorstep of abandonment and gives them a spiritual home, a name, and an identity — gives them sonship and an inheritance. He will be willing to go the distance with them through their ups and downs. He will be willing for them to wear his name, and he will share with them parts of his identity. He knows that if he strengthens them, covers them, and blesses them, part of who he is will reside in them.

This doesn't remove the spiritual children's own identity, but within their unique personality and identity, one will recognize traits and signs of who their spiritual father is. It's quite thrilling to see the fruit of such a relationship when all goes well. A connection with a true spiritual father gives sons and daughters an inheritance from which they will continue to receive ongoing blessing throughout their lives.

#6: Celebrates Their Children's Success

True spiritual parents desire that their children far exceed them in life, in money, in family, in ministry. They will not grow jealous or become angry that a spiritual son or daughter goes on to attain a more influential voice, a greater ministry outreach, or a larger financial base than they did.

A connection with a true spiritual father gives sons and daughters an inheritance from which they will continue to receive ongoing blessing throughout their lives.

That isn't true with slave masters. They start setting traps to throw the net of insecurity on those who are within their realm of authority, looking for an avenue of attack to lessen their impact and influence. But real spiritual fathers and mothers want their children to succeed and to go way beyond them.

#7: Prepares Children for Their Future

True spiritual parents are those who are able to see the future of their sons and daughters and to train them for it without letting them know what *they* know about their spiritual children's future until it's time.

I remember many times my mother and my grandmother would have me do certain things that established spiritual habits in my life when I was a young boy and even into my teenage years. And sometimes I'd wonder, *Why do I have to do this?*

But today I'm so thankful that my mom and grandma gave me a prayer life. I'm so glad they helped me establish habits for my life that I still have today in prayer, Bible reading, churchgoing, and morality. I'm so glad they gave me the love, training, discipline, and commands that I needed to grow into who I am today — and who I will continue to become to the glory of Christ for the rest of my life on this earth!

The Final Test: Self-Government

The final test before promotion is the test of self-governing. This is true for all believers, but it is certainly true before a mantle becomes secured for a person and great power is entrusted to him or her, because the lifestyle of a self-governed person is a visible sign of maturity.

God wants to know:

- Can He trust that person with a higher position of influence and with greater amounts of money?

- Can He trust that person to respond correctly when it's time to go through greater doors of opportunity and interact with people of influence and prestige?

- Can He trust that person to do His bidding when He sends him or her into difficult situations?

What is this quality of self-governing? In simple terms, it means that you will do what is right when no one is watching. God knows He can trust you to do what He asks you to do, no matter what environment you're in — whether one of applause or rejection — or what price you have to pay to do it.

You will be God's mouthpiece and will give the word of the Lord. You will pray for that person. You will give that amount of money He is prompting you to give. Regardless of the outcome of your obedience, even if it comes back on you as a negative or as an attack, you will do *whatever* the Lord is asking of you because you are in relationship with Him and you are governing yourself.

The lifestyle of a self-governed person is a visible sign of maturity. What is this quality of self-governing? In simple terms, it means that you will do what is right when no one is watching.

Self-governing starts with governing your body — all of its appetites and wants. Self-governing also deals with your mind. You must govern your intellect, your will, your emotions, your memory, and your imagination by continually renewing your mind with the Word of God. No matter what is going on in your life, you still pray; you still speak according to the Word. You don't give up; you don't get mad at God. You still believe, and you keep walking forward.

This is the ultimate outcome of good spiritual parenting — to raise mature sons and daughters who fit this description: those who are self-governing over their prayer life, their study of the Word, their morals, their money, their families, and their businesses or ministries. They have made obedience to God a lifestyle because they govern and discipline themselves to do what is right when no one is watching.

That's why some biological children who are actually called to succeed their parents' ministries haven't done it successfully — because they weren't self-governing. And in this season of a great generational changing of the guard in the Body of Christ, many are nervous about some sons and daughters succeeding certain fathers and mothers in the ministry.

It is somewhat like the days of Samuel and Eli (*see* Chapter 19). Sometimes a thought crosses people's minds, such as, *That son isn't quite right in his walk with God,* or, *Their daughter isn't living the way she is supposed to live.* As a result, there is a nervousness throughout the Body as some anticipate different ministries possibly getting off track once the children are put in charge. That kind of situation sometimes occurs when the parents didn't do what was required in earlier days — when they had the authority and strength within them to teach, train, and correct their sons and daughters until their children reached the level of maturity to self-govern.

**This is the ultimate outcome
of good spiritual parenting —
to raise mature sons and daughters
who fit this description: those who are self-governing
over their prayer life, their study of the Word,
their morals, their money, their families,
and their businesses or ministries.**

Only from that place of self-governing do spiritual sons and daughters come into their own, prepared to succeed the last generation and step into their divine assignment. When a spiritual son or daughter passes the test of self-governance, the elder generation can know they have finished their course well. The spiritual parent is able to hand off the mantle that is upon him or her to the one God has called to be the successor, knowing that the power and anointing of the mantle will only increase to become a double or a triple portion in the next generation.

The goal of every natural and spiritual parent is to get their spiritual children to this place of being self-governing. Parents want to have the trust, confidence, and assurance that the child will choose what is right in every situation, whether or not the parents are present. Self-governance is an essential quality for every believer, no matter what he or she is called to do — and it is absolutely essential for one called to inherit a mantle.

Only from that place of self-governing do
spiritual sons and daughters come into their own,
prepared to succeed the last generation
and step into their divine assignment.

'MY FATHER, MY FATHER!'

Consider all the characteristics we have just discussed about true spiritual parenting. *This* is what Elisha was saying when he said, "My father, my father!"

For the last ten years or so of Elijah's life, Elisha had served the man of God, his spiritual father. And as the two men walked together, engaging in daily interactions, Elijah's words penetrated Elisha's heart to set his foundation, align his character, and teach him how to grow up and do things properly.

Elijah told the younger prophet, "Here's how you do it. Don't go that way — go *this* way." Elijah trained Elisha so that when it came time for the spiritual son to receive the mantle, a strong foundation of character was already established. The needed understanding was there.

Elisha received Elijah as a father, not just as a prophetic person who gave him gifts and brought glory clouds in the room. And when the time was right, a great and beautiful transition took place.

**Elijah trained Elisha so that when it came time
for the spiritual son to receive the mantle,
a strong foundation of character was already established.
The needed understanding was there.**

Chapter 10

Portrait of a Spiritual Father

I can offer you a glimpse into the nature of a true spiritual father because of the relationship God gave me with Dr. Lester Sumrall. Although I was not the inheritor of Brother Sumrall's mantle, I did receive a powerful impartation for ministry and the help I needed at a critical juncture as a result of the role that this man of God occupied in my life.

Brother Sumrall was one who wouldn't stop at just helping his spiritual sons learn how to flow with the anointing. He knew it wouldn't be that difficult for a minister to tap into a flow of the Holy Ghost and cause the power of God to show up. But Dr. Sumrall was more interested in teaching his spiritual kids character and self-governance.

That's what true spiritual fathers and mothers do. They go to work on the character of their spiritual children, which is going to take more time than developing their giftings. This approach requires more of a personal touch at a closer range of ministry.

That goes along with another key quality of true spiritual parents that we talked about: They are *not* those who always agree with their spiritual children. The truth is, one who always agrees and never deals with problem issues can be a sign of a counterfeit spiritual parent.

There has to be a willingness on the part of spiritual fathers and mothers to commit themselves to the self-sacrifice and time-consuming responsibility of having their spiritual children in their lives. Sons and daughters consume much, much time.

**That's what true spiritual fathers and mothers do.
They go to work on the character
of their spiritual children, which is going
to take more time than developing their giftings.**

That was the beauty of Dr. Sumrall. There were many young ministers who truly needed the guidance and care of a spiritual father. Many had been wounded by others or had stumbled as a result of their own weaknesses. The elders who might have fulfilled the parenting role in their lives weren't available; perhaps they didn't want to take the time to do what needed to be done.

But then Dr. Sumrall would enter the picture, and he *would* take the time to help those younger ministers. He would accept the responsibility of being a spiritual father in their lives. Brother Sumrall would be able to see beyond the present fault, mistake, or pain to what needed to be done. He would patch up and do whatever was required — preach for them, call on them, pray for them — to get them set back on the road and moving forward again to fulfilling God's call on their lives.

A SPIRITUAL SON'S PERSONAL TESTIMONY

I can attest to this: Lester Sumrall was a good spiritual dad, because those whose lives he touched — those I am aware of — are still preaching today. And he was that kind of spiritual dad for me during a season in my early years of ministry when I was going through great hurt and pain in my life. Brother Sumrall took the time to walk through the hard times with me when I was about ready to quit.

This was in my early years of ministry in the late 1980s. I had already gone through different kinds of wars within the Body and had just come to the place where I said, "I'm tired; I'm done. Preachers are a mess." That's where I was at the time. I was hurt and disappointed, and I was shutting down.

I'd already been accepted to a university out in New England. I was going to go back to my birth name before my stepfather adopted me, which was Roberts Craft, so people couldn't track me down as Liardon and bother me. I was going to go back to an old identity and live happily ever after. I had already been accepted as a prospective student.

I was just very wounded. People had stolen money from me, lied about me, and "done me dirty." Church folks I'd known growing up as a boy — some whose ministries I had happily contributed to from my lawn-mowing money — had criticized me on public platforms.

I wasn't prepared for it all, because I had grown up in a family where what was said could be depended on to be the truth. My mom and grandma never lied to me, so I was very naïve in some ways. This experience brought a rude revelation of how some can be used by the enemy to land a devastating blow. I just didn't have the inner strength or capacity to work through it at that time.

I had already had my first visit to Dr. Sumrall in South Bend, Indiana, which I told you about in Chapter 3. So when I was at the point of almost shutting down, I had the thought, *Maybe Brother Sumrall can help me. I'll give him a chance.*

So I called Brother Sumrall on the phone. I reminded him, "Brother Sumrall, this is Roberts. If you remember, we have preached together at a number of conventions here in America and in Europe, and I came to visit you at your South Bend office awhile back."

I continued, "Brother Sumrall, I'm hurt, and I'm on my way out of ministry. I know it's probably not right, but I just can't stop the side of me that wants to quit right now because of the way I feel. The hurt is stronger than the will to keep going. Can you help me?"

"What seems to be the problem?" Brother Sumrall asked.

"Well, I don't like anyone who calls himself a preacher or who wants to be one. I know that my feelings are not right, but it's where I am at right now. I cannot keep holding those feelings on the inside and stay in the ministry. I need help."

"Well, get on a plane right now and come to South Bend. I'll be in my office waiting."

I protested, "But I can't be there until about 11 p.m., even if everything's on time."

'I'll be in my office," Brother Sumrall responded. "Come to the back door of the church, and I'll let you in."

So I got on the next flight. When I arrived late that night, I knocked on the back door, and true to his word, Brother Sumrall opened the door. He said, "I've been waiting for you." He led me into his office, sat down, and said, "Now talk to me."

I said, "I'm going to say it the way I feel it, and I'm not going to try to hold back anything." And then I "let 'er rip"! I roasted people's backsides; I called a few people some choice names. I figured it was my one opportunity to share what had been pent-up inside me, so I might as well lay it all out on the table.

Brother Sumrall just sat there, looking me in the eyes and listening. He was such a good man. He had a gruff exterior, but the heart of a father.

I went on for about an hour or so and finally didn't have anything else to say. Brother Sumrall leaned on the desk, resting his face on his hands, and asked me, "Are you done yet?"

Brother Sumrall just sat there,
looking me in the eyes and listening.
He was such a good man. He had a gruff exterior,
but the heart of a father.

I replied, "Well, I think I vented everything I know to say, and I said it how I wanted to say it."

Brother Sumrall answered, "All right, come over here and kneel down." When I did, he grabbed my head and began casting devils out of me.

I don't think those demons were just on me. I believe the hurt in my soul had built strongholds that had given access to demonic torment in my soul. So Brother Sumrall prayed for me to get rid of all the demonic oppression, and then he ministered in compassion to me.

Afterward, Brother Sumrall took me to the place they had prepared for me to stay. And he not only drove me there, but he went into the room with me and said, "All right, go to bed. I'm not going to leave until you're in bed. Then I'm going to turn off the light, and I'll be back to pick you up in the morning."

So while Brother Sumrall stood there, I got ready for bed, brushed my teeth, and got in bed. Then he said, "All right, now I'm in charge. Nothing will bother you tonight, and I'll see you in the morning."

The next morning, before I could even get my shoes tied, Brother Sumrall was at the door. "Are you ready to go?" he asked me when I opened the door.

I said, "Well, I'm here."

"Well, all right, today you're going to go with me all day long."

For the next two or three days, I was with Brother Sumrall in all that he did throughout each day — his TV shows, his finance meetings, etc. Throughout each day, he would walk with me, and right in the middle of doing something else, he'd stop and ask me, "Are you all right?"

"Yes, I'm good," I'd answer.

He'd reply, "Well, don't think too much. You're being healed. If you think, the wounds will open, so stop that. Just worship the Lord."

So Brother Sumrall got me through that difficult time, and we began to build a true bond and a close relationship based on great respect. Through that experience when I was struggling, he became a spiritual father to me. It was a father-son relationship that would only deepen in the following years until his graduation to Heaven in 1996.

When I started Spirit Life Bible College in California in the early '90s, Dr. Sumrall was one of our first guest speakers. He would come teach our students three times a year and was a frequent guest minister at our conventions. He loved me and my family and believed in the huge assignment God had given us.

Brother Sumrall got me through that difficult time,
and we began to build a true bond and
a close relationship based on great respect.
Through that experience when I was struggling,
he became a spiritual father to me.

I'd never really had a relationship with my natural father because he divorced my mother when I was a little boy. And by the time my mother married my stepfather, I was already in my teen years and my ministry had begun. So Brother Sumrall was really the first relationship in my life where I discovered what it was to experience both the compassion and the correction of a loving father.

HELPING A SON STAY ON TRACK

After I overcame that trial in those early years of my ministry and got back on the path God had ordained for me, my spiritual father still continued to counsel with me. When Brother Sumrall came to visit, he would tell me when I was right and he'd tell me when I was wrong.

"Now, don't be preaching that subject that way; it will cause problems."

"You're doing all right; keep preaching that, even if some don't like it."

"Why are you preaching that? Where did you get that from — some man or Jesus?"

Those are the kinds of questions a good spiritual father has to ask at times. He knows it is his responsibility to help a son get back on track when he has veered off in a way that could ultimately hurt him.

For instance, the Lord may ask a young minister to step into territory that is considered by some to be controversial. A spiritual father might need to step in if he sees that the son, in his own immaturity, begins to go off course by adopting an unwise approach of his own preference.

This happened to me during those early years of ministry when Brother Sumrall walked with me as a spiritual father. I learned that even if a minister is called to do certain things for God that some would call controversial, he has to make sure that the controversy is created by the right cause and not by some foolish distraction.

The subject of deliverance fits in that category. Casting out devils is part of the Gospel (*see* Mark 16:17). Deliverance at times is required. And my view is that whether a demon is in a person or on a person, let's just get rid of it! Being demon-free is a lot better than being "demon-hiding." Some protest, "I don't have any devils" — yet it's evident demons are sitting on them, picking away at their soul!

The Lord has given me a deliverance anointing that I've never been ashamed of. I'm not afraid of spiritual warfare. I'm not afraid of casting devils out of or off of whomever. Yet I also understand that sometimes what people call a devil is not a devil. It may be a flesh issue, or it could possibly be a hurt or a wound that needs to be healed.

I learned that even if a minister is called
to do certain things for God that some
would call controversial, he has to make sure
that the controversy is created by the right cause
and not by some foolish distraction.

But deliverance has always been a controversial issue in a lot of places, especially in the denominational world or in many Pentecostal churches. The general consensus is that people believe in deliverance as part of their church history but don't want it playing out in their present activity.

It's one thing to say, "I believe in deliverance because it's in my doctrine." But do you have it manifesting in your church and in your meetings when people are obviously needing to be delivered?

You're not trying to deliver people who don't need it, because not everyone is demonized. At times every believer will be tempted, and demonic powers will always try to find a foothold to gain access in order to harass and oppress. But that doesn't mean that every believer is always oppressed or needs to be delivered.

In the beginning stages of my relationship with Brother Sumrall, he said to me, "I want to know what you teach about deliverance." He had heard rumors that I believed everyone has demons and that there has to be a physical manifestation, such as a person throwing up, in order for that person to be delivered.

But I don't believe that. At times such things do occur; it happened in Jesus' ministry. Scriptures mention a demonized person who physically foamed at the mouth and whose flesh was torn and bruised by demons (*see* Luke 9:39). But such a manifestation is not true in every case.

So if such things happened at times in Jesus' earthly ministry, it may happen at times for a minister of the Gospel in *this* day. Of course, this isn't applicable in every situation, but many have said *no* to ministering deliverance in *any* situation.

Yet we don't have the option to just bow out of all deliverance ministry, because Jesus didn't do that! That means situations will arise that we will have to face and deal with. But we don't freak out; we just minister deliverance. And we focus on the point of deliverance — not on the name of the devil or on any manifestations that may have occurred leading to the point of deliverance. We focus on the person who has been set free!

So Brother Sumrall came to me and said, "Roberts, I've been hearing that you preach this weird demon doctrine."

I replied, "Well, I don't think I do, but let me tell you what I believe, because I got it from Norvel Hayes and you."

Lester Sumrall and Norvel Hayes are the two ministers who taught me how to deal with demons, because the members of the Pentecostal church I grew up in never taught on or talked about demons — even though a lot of them were being influenced or tormented by them! They might admit that Christians are supposed to cast out devils — but it was always the people in Africa who had demons, not anyone in America.

That is the attitude of a large portion of the American Church. Yet if we could see in the Spirit when we visit one of our nice American malls where folks go dressed up in trendy clothes and expensive shoes, we'd see demonic beings hanging on a whole crowd of them! Those are the ones we're sent to deliver, because they think the state they're in is normal! Thank God, Jesus will set them free and give them a true normal life.

(As a side note, I only skipped classes twice as a high school student: once when the original "Star Wars" movie first hit the theaters, and a second time when Norvel Hayes came to Tulsa and held a week-long seminar on casting out demons. I never got in trouble with my teachers, and I never regretted attending that seminar. As I launched into ministry soon afterward, what I had learned from Norvel about dealing with demons turned out to be invaluable!)

GROWING THROUGH
UNCOMFORTABLE MOMENTS

So Brother Sumrall said, "All right, tell me what you believe and give me examples of each one."

When Brother Sumrall interrogated you, it was very intimidating because he had a serious look and a "Hmmm" sound that went with the interrogation. And you didn't know if that was a good "Hmmm" or if you had just stated a wrong doctrinal belief!

This was all new to me, because I'd never had that type of inquiry done by someone outside of my family. But today I praise God for those uncomfortable moments, because I see what was taking place in the midst of it all: I was learning how to be a son to a father.

It was different when I was with my pastor, Billy Joe Daugherty (*see* Chapter 11). When I was with Billy Joe, I felt like I was loved and doing great, all things considered. The apostolic gruffness of someone such as Lester Sumrall was not part of Billy Joe's makeup.

Now, Brother Sumrall loved me, too, but he was an apostle. He was going to ask the hard questions: "What's going on in these situations? Is this doctrine being taught correctly? If you don't keep things in order, everyone gets weird." That's the way those who are called to the apostolic ministry think.

Today I praise God for those uncomfortable moments, because I see what was taking place in the midst of it all: I was learning how to be a son to a father.

Brother Sumrall was a world apostle who in that season of his life was fathering many young ministers, and there was a certain protocol for the young minister to follow when discussing matters with him. In this discussion about demonology, Brother Sumrall helped guide me through that process. He told me, "Give me an example for each point as you explain to me what you believe about this subject and how it has worked in your meetings."

So I went through my whole teaching on demonology, and Brother Sumrall didn't say one thing — just an occasional "Hmmm…," while his eyes looked into mine with an interrogating gaze as he listened. That's the way I remember it. My perception may have been more dramatic than it really was, but that's what it felt like to me — as if he were looking right through me.

As I talked, again and again I had the thought, *Maybe there was something wrong in how I said that.* That was the way it felt as I kept talking for 30 or 40 minutes, giving an overview of how I taught the subject of demonology. I also shared some examples of demonic manifestations that had happened in my meetings where I did my best in dealing with the situation.

When I was finished speaking, Dr. Sumrall finally spoke: "Well, there's nothing wrong with your doctrine."

I thought, *Oh, praise God, the "deliverance man" thinks my doctrines are right!*

That's how Brother Sumrall was known in our circles — as *the* authority on deliverance. He had helped the Word of Faith world become a little stronger and more aware and accepting of the need for deliverance, despite "the ditches" that some had fallen into concerning this area of ministry in the past. Many in the Body of Christ looked to Brother Sumrall with great respect as the "demon expert."

Brother Sumrall continued, "The problem with you is that you don't know how to communicate this subject right."

Then Brother Sumrall continued, "Another thing that you don't know how to do well is explain yourself. Instead of doing what is needed to explain why you minister the way you do, you get defensive. Too often young ministers get defensive when corrected, and that's why they get hurt and quit."

I thought, *Well, yes, that's what I did.*

Brother Sumrall continued, "You have a newsletter."

"Yes, sir."

"All right, in the next issue I want you to go through all the mail you've received about this controversy and pull out the questions. Include each question in the newsletter and answer each one. Then send me a copy of that newsletter."

"As I minister around the nation," Brother Sumrall continued, "when I hear somebody say anything about this subject, I will say, 'Well, here's what Roberts printed, and I've reviewed his doctrines. This should settle it for you.'"

I did what Brother Sumrall instructed; he did what he promised he would do; and the situation improved significantly over the next period of time. But one lesson I had to learn from it all was this: to follow Dr. Sumrall's counsel didn't mean I was compromising or backing down from what I believed was right. That's how I had sometimes seen correction up to that point, but that perspective was just the result of spiritual immaturity.

You see, maturity wants unity. I've always been a warrior ready for a good battle. But I had to learn that it must be for the right cause — for *God's* cause — not for matters of preference or for minor issues. And a key part of my learning process involved Brother Sumrall's fatherly dealing with problematic issues in my soul as he helped me yield to the Holy Spirit's work of removing what needed to go.

This is a process all sons must go through. It may at times feel like they are not being honored. However, the reality is that they are being adjusted and corrected to be made more perfect for their ministry to people. They are learning that ministry is to help people, not to divide people.

Of course, religion will always fight those who break out of its box to follow the Holy Spirit, so it's inevitable that certain battles will have to be fought. I asked Brother Sumrall about that during this discussion on dealing with demons. I said to him, "There are some places I go to preach where I'm not trying to be divisive, but it doesn't matter how I say the truth about this subject. I've tried to say it softly, and I've tried to say it loud, but my words just bounce back at me."

A key part of my learning process involved
Brother Sumrall's fatherly dealing with
problematic issues in my soul as he helped me
yield to the Holy Spirit's work
of removing what needed to go.
This is a process all sons must go through.

Brother Sumrall replied, "Well, there are certain subjects that no matter what you do, religion will always get mad at you. Deliverance is one of them. And you can go to some churches, and it doesn't matter *what* you say about *anything* — to them it will be wrong. So just accept that this is the way it is with some folks.

"But we're not talking about that right now," Brother Sumrall said to me. "We're talking about folks who want to believe in you and run with you. If you will follow my counsel, you'll have done your part to resolve their questions and issues, and there will be more who will accept you."

THE HARVEST OF A SPIRITUAL FATHER

I found out from preachers around Europe and from some in America that Dr. Sumrall would tell them to invite me to minister. He'd say, "You need him, because he's a future leader."

He wouldn't say that to my face, but he'd say it to preachers, and they'd tell me later.

I would call Dr. Sumrall whenever I needed him, and he'd take the call. I'd say, "I need to come see you," and he'd make himself available so we could talk. I was corrected by Brother Sumrall many times, and I was loved by him always. It was a true father-son relationship — one that I miss greatly.

Today I look back over my years of ministry since I was blessed to spend time with my spiritual father, and I can honestly make this statement: As I followed Brother Sumrall's counsel in the areas of my life that faced his loving correction, I benefited every time.

I was corrected by Brother Sumrall many times, and I was loved by him always. It was a true father-son relationship — one that I miss greatly.

Lester Sumrall would welcome the young ministers to his office and spend time with them. I'd be with him sometimes in Eastern Germany, and he'd be ministering at a convention of 50 people — and then he'd return the next year to minister to the same 50 people. Brother Sumrall didn't go for the crowd; he went for the young men and women he had met who needed fathering. He'd go and spend time with them.

Brother Sumrall once told me, "I've always had to get a new group of friends every time I make a transition. Most of the friends I ran with in the last wave don't like all of you young stallions in the ministry — but I do. I'm called to be with you, to help you stay on the straight and narrow and do what is right, to encourage you and impart to you necessary wisdom."

And that's what my spiritual father did for me. Brother Sumrall imparted so much valuable wisdom to me over the years I knew him. I have in my vault a private little book I wrote that contains nuggets and stories that he related to me over the years.

The last time Dr. Sumrall preached for us in Irvine, he preached on "Good-bye, Earth, it's been nice knowing you." It was his farewell sermon. When we got back to the hotel after the service, he waited until he was alone in the car with me; then he said, "I can't come back to your church."

My first thought was, *What in the world did I do to cause this? What happened?*

Dr. Sumrall went on to explain, "I can't come back because I'm going to Heaven soon. You can come visit me anywhere, but I will not be able to make it back, because I'm leaving."

Dr. Sumrall encouraged me, saying, "Keep telling the story to the next generation of the past generations of generals and pioneers for God. It's one way you transfer faith. You've got to tell the right stories." Then he gave me that blessing. And his last prayer was how he always prayed for me, speaking those two commanding words: *"Be blessed!"*

That was Dr. Sumrall's last time to California and the last time I actually saw him in person, although I talked to him on the phone a few more times. He graduated to Heaven about eight months later in April 1996.

I thank God for this general who was willing to walk with me as a father. He didn't receive public accolades or applause for the spiritual parenting that I or others received from him all those years. But years after Brother Sumrall passed on to Heaven, his reward lives on through the commitment of his spiritual kids to live honorably and wisely before the Lord, to faithfully pursue what God has called them to do, and to speak of their spiritual father with honor.

When godly men and women of Dr. Lester Sumrall's caliber finish their course and graduate to Heaven, a huge void is felt in the hearts of so many in the Kingdom. I know this to be true, because when he passed on, that void was deeply felt by this spiritual son.

Years after Brother Sumrall passed on to Heaven, his reward lives on through the commitment of his spiritual kids to live honorably and wisely before the Lord, to faithfully pursue what God has called them to do, and to speak of their spiritual father with honor.

For all the days of my life on this earth and beyond into eternity, the deposit of Brother Sumrall's spirit that he imparted to me will be a part of my internal makeup — and that deposit will be passed on to all of my own spiritual sons and daughters. I will always speak of him with honor, respect, and a deep sense of gratitude. That is one way spiritual sons bring honor to the house of their father.

Chapter 11

THE VITAL ROLE
OF A PASTOR

I want to give you one more example of this process of correction and adjustment that is so necessary in the fulfilling of divine purpose. Since my walk with the Lord is the one I know best, I'll draw on a key moment in my life one more time and share from my relationship with my pastor, Pastor Billy Joe Daugherty of Victory Christian Center in Tulsa. Billy Joe was my pastor for almost 30 years, from the time I was a teenager until he graduated to Heaven in 2009.

Before I go on, let me interject a key truth right here: *Every person needs a pastor.* That includes *every* minister who stands in any of the fivefold ministry offices, including one called to inherit a mantle. The importance of a pastor's role in every person's life can't be overstated.

This is vital for me to stress in this discussion about mantles, because so many ministers think they don't need a pastor. In fact, some ministers who stand in the prophetic or apostolic offices erroneously conclude that the pastoral office is a "lower" office and that pastors therefore need to submit to *them*.

But that is unscriptural. God intended that *every* person be submitted to a pastor as a stabilizing force in his or her life.

The Spirit of God will move on the one called to pastor you to point out certain aspects of your life that need adjustment. Your pastor will tell you at times, "This needs to be dealt with. It is more important than you think it is."

Some may view a pastor's correction as offensive or feel like their pastor is disrespecting them when he begins to deal with stumbling blocks that they consider to be no big deal or a private matter.

But that is actually one way we will see the love of the Father God in action — when a pastor's love causes him to step across the line of privacy and enter our world. A pastor does it not for the sake of embarrassing or exposing us in a wrong way, but to deal with issues that must be dealt with. A true pastor's heart is that before we set out to fulfill what God has called us to do, hindrances would be removed so they don't become stumbling blocks for us or for those around us.

God intended that *every* person
be submitted to a pastor as a stabilizing force
in his or her life.

A Pastor's Help

That is certainly the role Pastor Billy Joe filled in my life. I'll give you an example. One day he sat down with me with a specific purpose in mind: He saw that I needed an adjustment in how I was teaching a certain subject.

Billy Joe said, "I'm going to share with you a rule for ministers, Roberts. We want the message we're preaching to be effective in people's lives. So if we have to change semantics in order for people to receive the divine deposit into their hearts, we're going to do it. As for you, if you'll just use biblical terms and not create new terms that can be misunderstood, you'll avoid a lot of trouble."

Billy Joe continued, "A lot of the controversies ministers are getting into arise not so much from saying something wrong in principle; it is in the semantics they use. That's the terrain of the present Church that we have to navigate at this moment in time."

When my pastor first said that to me, it provoked an arrogance that lurked in my immature mind. I heard what he said and accepted it as something I had to do. But in my mind, I still had an attitude of, *Ugh! Let the ones who don't like my semantics work it out. I don't see anything wrong with how I'm saying things!* That attitude is what the Holy Spirit was working at. He was helping me learn to die to my flesh as the Word kept being sown into my life.

Billy Joe Daugherty was a wonderful man. He would see me every so often and say, "Praise God, you've got that lesson down, haven't you, Roberts?"

I'd answer, "Yes, Pastor, I've got it."

But I hadn't really gotten that lesson settled in my heart. I was obeying my pastor's admonition, but in my heart, I wasn't totally there yet. It took me a little while to work through it and come to the conclusion that my attitude was arrogant. I finally realized that I was being young and foolish in wanting to hold on to my opinion in the matter.

A PASTOR'S CORRECTION
IS AN ACT OF HONOR AND LOVE

And I want to emphasize this point: When our pastor deals with issues that are hindering us in our lives, it is a true act of honor and love, even though it doesn't always feel like that to us when we're receiving correction.

In the example I gave above from my relationship with Billy Joe Daugherty, I can tell you with certainty that my pastor was 100 percent *for* me during the three decades he pastored me before he went on to Heaven. He was proud that I graduated from his high school and was a part of his church.

What if I had allowed myself to get offended? What if in my arrogance I had backed off from the alignment, covering, and blessing that Pastor Billy Joe and his wife Sharon had been to me for so many years just because I felt put down when he dealt with an issue in my life? I would have suffered a huge loss, and I would have had no one to blame but myself.

If we don't humble ourselves to admit that we could be wrong when our pastor or our spiritual father comes to counsel and correct, pride will keep us from growing. Pride stops growth and gives us an air of being a know-it-all when, in actuality, we don't know what we don't know.

The process I went through in that example is simply called growing up in God with the help of my Heaven-appointed pastor. We all must go through that process — and certainly that includes the successor to a mantle.

**If we don't humble ourselves
to admit that we could be wrong when our pastor
or our spiritual father comes to counsel and correct,
pride will keep us from growing.**

and gives us an air of being a know it all when, in actuality, we don't know what we don't know.

The process I went through in that example is simply called growing up in God with the help of my Heaven-appointed pastor. We all must go through that process — and certainly that includes the successor to a mantle.

If we don't humble ourselves
to admit that we could be wrong when our pastor,
or our spiritual father urges to counsel and correct,
pride will keep us from growing.

Chapter 12

ELISHA AND ELIJAH: THE UNFOLDING JOURNEY

L et's return to the account of Elijah and Elisha one last time. A prophetic picture is provided us in 2 Kings chapters 2 and 3 of how the parenting relationship unfolds when divine order is in place.

As Elisha accompanied his spiritual father on his last journey, refusing to leave his side, Elijah traveled through three different cities — Gilgal, Bethel, and Jericho — before arriving at the Jordan River. The spiritual significance of these four stops on Elijah's journey is worth mentioning in our discussion of mantles and the importance of the spiritual father-son relationship.

GILGAL:
THE FIRST STEP

Elijah and Elisha began their journey in Gilgal (*see* 2 Kings 2:1), a city mentioned 39 times in the Bible. Gilgal was the place where the Israelites set up camp after the miraculous crossing of the Jordan River. There they set up a memorial of 12 stones to remind them and the generations to come of what the Lord had done for them (*see* Joshua 4:19-20).

Later it was the place where Joshua commanded the rite of circumcision to be restored, and the reproach of Egypt was rolled off the Israelites as they were brought back into covenant with their God (*see* Joshua 5:7-9). Hence, the city was called Gilgal, which means *rolling*.

The fact that Elijah's journey with Elisha began in Gilgal symbolically represents the first step that a spiritual son or daughter must take in their training: They must covenant to rid themselves of the flesh and of all selfish ambition. Elisha was successful in doing that. The next generation of spiritual son in training was Gehazi in his service to Elisha. As we will discuss in Chapter 19, Gehazi ultimately failed the test by yielding to the sin of covetousness (*see* 2 Kings 5:17-27).

BETHEL:
LEARNING THE WAYS OF GOD

Next, Elijah and Elisha passed through Bethel, which means *the house of God* (*see* 2 Kings 2:2-3). Altars were built at Bethel by Abraham and then later by Jacob (*see* Gen. 12:8; 35:7). People went there to seek God in troubled times. Deborah held her courts there as judge and governor of Israel (*see* Judges 4:5). Later King Josiah destroyed the high places of pagan worship in Bethel (*see* 2 Kings 23:19).

Bethel, being the house of God, symbolically represents a place where a son learns the ways of God. This is the part of the journey where the son learns how God works and what ways of working are accepted or rejected by Him.

Therefore, Bethel represents a time of walking with the mantle carrier. This will usually involve a time of working together in person, although that is not always possible. Regardless, the son must learn from the father how covenant works, because every one of these mantles work according to certain rules of engagement.

A person cannot just jump on a stage and begin to conduct a miracle service the way Kathryn Kuhlman did. There are milestones in God concerning one's dedication, consecration, and the dealing with one's flesh that must be reached over a period of time in order to be trusted with great power and anointing. Bethel, then, represents a place or a season of life where the spiritual son or daughter begins to learn the ways of cooperating with the Lord.

There are milestones in God
concerning one's dedication, consecration,
and the dealing with one's flesh that must be reached
over a period of time in order to be trusted
with great power and anointing.

JERICHO:
THE PLACE OF BATTLE

Elijah and Elisha then traveled from Bethel to Jericho (*see* 2 Kings 2:4-5). Jericho was a pagan center of moon worship.

Some scholars add the meaning that Jericho then denotes a place of emotion. Also, some scholars attribute the meaning of scent or fragrance to Jericho because of the fragrant trees that were common in the city during that time.

However, the meaning connected to Jericho that seems most significant to me is that this ancient city was a place of *battle*.

There is a warfare factor that a person must live with when carrying a mantle. There's no on/off button he or she can push; it is a constant battle.

Satan assigns principalities — not just minor demons — to wage war against these top mantle carriers. I'm referring here to the dominant, national-impact mantles. These are demonic beings that rule cities and go after mantles. It's a whole different level of spiritual warfare. These principalities have been working at their assignment for a long time, and they're just waiting for an opportunity to derail and destroy. Therefore, the warfare of a mantle carrier is much more intense and continuous than the spiritual battles most believers face.

There is a warfare factor that a person must live with when carrying a mantle. There's no on/off button he or she can push; it is a constant battle.

For instance, why did Aimee Semple MacPherson go through all the trouble she experienced in her life and ministry (*see* Chapter 15)? It is evident that she was dealing with an uncommon level of satanic opposition. There was a demonic assignment at work, intent on stopping that healing mantle from functioning.

Satan assigns certain principalities with an ongoing task of buffeting that particular mantle assignment in every generation. They are to find the weaknesses of the mantle carriers and exploit them.

We'll discuss in the following chapters how this principle has played out over the past few generations each time this top healing mantle has fit upon a human vessel. In each generation, the enemy found an inroad to attack the mantle carrier in the areas of marriage and the physical heart. That sounds crazy to some, but to me it's as clear as a bell.

Satan assigns certain principalities with an ongoing task
of buffeting that particular mantle assignment
in every generation. They are to find the weaknesses
of the mantle carriers and exploit them.

JORDAN RIVER:
LEARNING THE ANOINTING

Finally, Elijah and Elisha reached the Jordan River (*see* 2 Kings 2:6). The Hebrew word for *Jordan* means *down* and gives a picture of a river *flowing down* a mountain. Psalm 133:3 likens the anointing to the dew from Mt. Hermon flowing down to the valley below.

The river that forms from that dew is the Jordan River, so in this journey of Elijah and Elisha, the Jordan represents the anointing of God and necessity of the son to learn to work and cooperate with that anointing. It was there at the river that Elisha saw Elijah perform his last miracle, when the elder prophet struck the water with his mantle and the river divided to allow them to cross on dry ground (*see* 2 Kings 2:8).

So Elijah and Elisha's last journey together to these four destinations before Elijah was taken away to Heaven paints a vivid picture of the journey of a spiritual father and son — a crucial part of the process before the passing of a mantle. Along the path from disciple to successor, the son learns:

1. To cut away the flesh.

2. To walk in the ways of God.

3. How to wage war.

4. How to flow in and work with the anointing.

All of these lessons are crucial steps leading to the moment at the end of the journey. Only when these steps are fulfilled is the mature son ready to receive his divine inheritance and take up the father's mantle.

God's Generals in *Mantles Past and Present* (in order of mention)

George Jeffreys
Healing Evangelist
1889 - 1962

George Jeffreys
with his Bible

Reinhard Bonnke with
Roberts Liardon and Roberts'
mother, Carol Liardon

Reinhard Bonnke
Healing Evangelist
1940 - 2019

Reinhard Bonnke
preaching at massive crusade in Africa

Smith Wigglesworth
"Apostle of Faith"
1859 - 1947

Smith reading his Bible

Dr. Lester Sumrall
Apostle, Pastor, and Evangelist
1913 - 1996

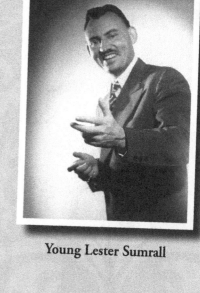

Young Lester Sumrall

Dr. Sumrall and Roberts
Spiritual dad and son

Dr. Oral Roberts
Healing Evangelist
1918 - 2009

Oral Roberts with the Liardon family
at Carol Liardon's ORU graduation
in 1973

Roberts Liardon and
Oral Roberts

Oral ministering to a woman
at a healing crusade

Roberts with Pastors Sharon and
Billy Joe Daugherty at a Spirit Life Bible College
graduation in Irvine, CA

Billy Joe Daugherty
1952 - 2009
Pastor of Victory Christian Center
Tulsa, OK

Pastor Billy Joe Daugherty and
Roberts Liardon

Maria Woodworth-Etter
Healing Evangelist
1844 - 1924

Mother Etter with her Bible

MARIA WOODWORTH-ETTER
"MIRACLE TENT"

Aimee Semple McPherson
Healing Evangelist
1890 - 1944

Aimee praying for a sick woman

Aimee ministering to a bedfast patient

Kathryn Kuhlman
Healing Evangelist
1907 - 1976

Kathryn Kuhlman ministering

William Branham
Prophet
1909 - 1965

William Branham
in his latter years

Chapter 13

A 'Mantle Tour' Through Three Generations

In the next three chapters, I want to take you on a three-generational tour of a top healing mantle so you can see how a mantle operates and how it is fought. This particular healing mantle that we're going to talk about is one of the more significant in America's history.

I have found in my studies on God's generals over the years that when God wants a certain aspect of His kindness and His miracle-working power to be demonstrated considerably in the eyes of the people of a nation, He will highlight a person with that gifting. Often that person will receive widespread attention as his or her anointing and gifting speak to the national consciousness. In such a case, dominion and authority help make up the fabric, but the mantle is the cloth.

There were two dominant works of Jesus while He was on this earth that God wants to keep continually in the consciousness of the Body of Christ and of this nation: He *saved*, and He *healed*. It's possible to therefore track through the generations both a great national salvation mantle and a national healing mantle in the United States of America.

When God wants a certain aspect
of His kindness and His miracle-working power
to be demonstrated considerably
in the eyes of the people of a nation,
He will highlight a person with that gifting.
In such a case, dominion and authority
help make up the fabric, but the mantle is the cloth.

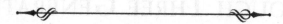

THE GREAT AMERICAN HEALING MANTLE

For the purpose of this discussion, I want to focus in these next three chapters on the story of three generations of a mantle that I call the great American healing mantle.

God wants a healing ministry to be part of the national conscience of America. Of course, any believer can pray for the sick, and some people have a special gifting for healing. But this particular mantle is national in scope and known for its sustained dramatic and miraculous demonstration of God's healing power. This mantle can be traced through three generations and helps us understand how those who carried the mantle operated in their giftings.

This healing mantle came to Kathryn Kuhlman, who received it from Aimee McPherson, who inherited it from Maria Woodworth-Etter. I believe that the inception of this national healing mantle occurred with Maria's ministry in the late 1800s, so that is where our journey through three generations of mantle carriers will begin.

COMMON THREADS

As you read on, you will notice several common threads interwoven throughout these three women's lives and ministries. I'll highlight just a few to look for at the outset.

- Each woman faced persecution as she stepped out to answer her call.

- The color white appeared in each generation as the color each woman most often chose to wear when ministering. We'll see that for Aimee, there was a specific reason for this, but the common reason for all three women was that white depicts holiness and purity.

- The signs and wonders that manifested in each woman's ministry eventually attracted national attention.

- Each woman was popular with the general public and the press in the beginning, only to see both later turn on her and act as adversaries.

- Each woman faced marital difficulties that ultimately led to divorce.

- Each woman suffered some kind of loss in the area of children.

- Each would also deal with some kind of heart issue
  that later became a contributing factor in her death.

You can see from several common threads in that list that
these three generations of women preachers had to deal with an
unseen enemy that fought this healing mantle. Satan does *not*
want this healing mantle active and effective on the earth, and
through the years, he has employed similar strategies to stop it.

With that said, let's begin our "tour" of the great American
healing mantle through its first three generations. This brief
overview of the ministries of these three remarkable women
is truly a testimony of mighty demonstration of God's power
despite all opposition, all to His glory and honor.[6]

---

[6] *Note:* You can find a more detailed account of the lives of these three women generals
in my first volume of *God's Generals* and in my books *Maria Woodworth-Etter: The Complete Collection of Her Life Teachings* and *Kathryn Kuhlman: A Spiritual Biography of God's
Miracle Worker.*

Chapter 14

America's Top Healing Mantle 1st Generation: Maria Woodworth-Etter

A woman was brought forth on a cot, bedfast since childhood. After laying hands on her and with boldness and a great shout, Maria declared her healed and told her to get up. The woman attempted to get up but lay back down. Maria gave the charge again: "The Lord of Heaven commands you to rise!" This time she did.

First she grabbed the rails of her cot and pulled herself to a seated position; then she suddenly got up from the cot. The crowd stood and rushed the scene to verify the healing. But they didn't have to worry about getting a good view; Maria picked the woman up in her arms, carrying her up to the pulpit to testify.

And the woman did, according to reports. She wept and spoke fervently about the Lord. It was reported that she went home completely restored and proved it by doing a full day's washing and ironing.[7]

GRANDMOTHER OF THE PENTECOSTAL MOVEMENT

Mother Etter (as she was called in her latter years of ministry) was God's chosen vessel to be an influential voice to America in restoring the revelation that healing is part of Christ's redemption. She was such a strong woman of vision and spiritual strength.

Mother Etter was chosen by God to carry His light into darkness. She discerned and caught the wave of the Pentecostal Movement as it began to rise from the still waters of the Holiness Movement. In fact, Maria Woodworth-Etter is known as the "grandmother of the Pentecostal Movement" because she had all nine gifts of the Spirit in operation — including speaking in tongues — before Azuza Street. Throughout most of her long years of ministry, she embraced, walked in, and taught extensively on the Pentecostal experience.[8]

Those qualities didn't come automatically to Maria. They were forged in the fire of great trials and opposition that began in her younger years and continued on through the decades of her ministry. But Maria's love for Jesus prevailed and pushed through every challenge. Throughout her ministry, she stood strong in the face of everything that opposed and allowed the Holy Spirit to spread His fire through her.

---

[7] Roberts Liardon, *Maria Woodworth-Etter: A God's Generals Resource* (Harrison House Publishers, Kindle Edition), pp. 24-25.
[8] Ibid., p. 38.

**Mother Etter was God's chosen vessel
to be an influential voice to America
in restoring the revelation that healing
is part of Christ's redemption.**

OVERCOMING A 'MAN-FEARING SPIRIT' TO ANSWER GOD'S CALL

Maria Woodworth-Etter was born in 1844 and saved at a young age. She almost immediately sensed the call of God on her life to the ministry. She could hear God's voice calling her again and again, asking her to step out and preach the Word. She fought that voice but not from a rebellious heart. In those early years of her walk with Christ, Maria was infected with the disease that has stopped many from taking a crucial step of obedience: She was afraid — held back by what she called a "man-fearing" spirit. It was a fear fueled by the prevailing belief in her Christian circles that women couldn't preach.

Yet the call of God burned relentlessly in this young woman's heart. When Maria was 13 years old, she was caught up in a vision that would prove to be pivotal in the years to come. In the vision, she stood in a wheat field and saw the sheaves of wheat fall down around her, and the Lord said, *"The slaying of the Lord shall be many."*

At the time, Maria thought the vision represented the salvation of souls, which it did in part. But it also pictured the slaying power of the Holy Ghost that would one day help define her ministry.

In those early years of her walk with Christ, Maria was infected with the disease that has stopped many from taking a crucial step of obedience: She was afraid — held back by what she called a "man-fearing" spirit.

After the Civil War, young Maria married Philo H. Woodworth, a Civil War veteran, and together they thought to make an honest living from the land as farmers. But as it turned out, the couple couldn't even keep their chickens or their hogs alive.

Then over a period of several years, five of the Woodworths' six children died young, one by one, from sickness. Maria herself struggled with sickness and at times hovered between death and life. During these episodes, she would have visions at times of Heaven and of herself pleading with sinners to get saved. The Lord was preparing Maria to answer the call to ministry that she couldn't escape.

When the Woodworths' fifth child died, leaving only one child living — their daughter Lizzie — the deep anguish that Maria struggled with became her wakeup call. She realized that nothing was working in their lives, and she knew she still had to face the call that had burned in her heart since she first began walking with Jesus.

**The Lord was preparing Maria to answer
the call to ministry that she couldn't escape.**

Although Maria's husband seemed to be in agreement with her decision to answer her call to the ministry in the beginning, his heart became hardened in time, possibly as a result of all the loss they had experienced. But for Maria, there could be no backing out of the "yes" she had finally said to the Lord.

Maria pursued ordination through what we call a small ministerial network today. This feisty little woman was only 5 foot 2 inches, but every time she heard a "no," she just kept saying, "Oh, yes, I will!"

MAKING THE HARD GROUND YIELD FRUIT

The push-and-pull between the leaders of the ministerial network and Maria went on for a while. But, finally, the organization decided to ordain Maria so they didn't have to keep dealing with her persistent asking. They didn't know they were about set the nation set on fire and see whole cities impacted by the power of God as a result of that one decision!

The ministerial organization gave Maria tasks that no other minister wanted, assigning her to plow hard ground and to work on reviving dead or dying congregations in the surrounding area. (This would actually become a key part of her mantle assignment — breaking up dry, hard spiritual ground and preparing the way for whatever God had planned next for that particular territory.) Maria was even given the task of bringing revival to the most terrible place for Gospel activity in the entire region at that time — a place aptly nicknamed "Devil's Den."

Bringing revival in a spiritually dead place like Devil's Den may have intimidated the average preacher, but not Maria. It's what God had anointed her to accomplish! She'd just do what she knew to do — hold a revival. And whereas those who had gone there before her couldn't draw a crowd or get anyone saved, Maria would come in and pack out the place the first night!

Hundreds came to see Maria. People thought, *A woman can't preach!* During the first several days, they'd mock her when she got up to preach. But then the power of God began to break out, and the mockery petered out. After several days of revival meetings, a breakthrough began to happen, and God turned that thing around. In the end, Maria Woodworth-Etter had built a church of 200 people and established a Sunday school there. By the time she was done, she had made the place a "Christ house" instead of a devil's den!

Bringing revival in a spiritually dead place like Devil's Den may have intimidated the average preacher, but not Maria. It's what God had anointed her to accomplish!

In the process, the group who had vilified Maria experienced a change of heart. They actually came back to her and apologized, telling her, "We did you wrong, and we're so sorry we were against you, now that we see your fruit." The people got behind Maria, and eventually she built more churches in that region than all their preachers put together. A woman did that! But Maria wasn't just any woman. She was a fiery, anointed preacher with all nine gifts of the Spirit operating through her before anyone had ever heard of the Azusa Outpouring!

Initially, it was the oddity of a woman preaching that drew most of the town to see it. They couldn't believe that a woman was going to try to preach. They didn't have cell phones and movies and online streaming, so the woman preacher was the town entertainment!

"Are you going to go see the woman preach tonight? My whole block is going out to the show! We'll see you there!" So people would all show up to see a spectacle; Maria would preach the salvation message of the Lord by the anointing of God; and people would respond and keep coming back!

THE REWARD OF PRESSING THROUGH

Those early years of ministry were difficult for the petite woman preacher. She would travel long miles by horseback from place to place, and her fiery preaching would compel people to come to the altar to get saved. Then she'd return to take care of her responsibilities at the family farm.

Meanwhile, the heart of Maria's husband became more and more hardened and bitter. By the late 1880s, Maria and Philo were separated. Philo was drinking, sleeping with women who came to the meetings, and sometimes actively trying to stop her meetings.

In 1891 during one of Maria's meetings in California, her husband divorced her and ran off with one of the ladies in the city. Within a year of the divorce, Philo Woodworth died of typhoid fever.[9]

Maria's steadfastness and stamina is amazing to me. She just kept right on going and preached through this whole process of betrayal and divorce. Whatever daunting challenge she was given or however weary she felt in meeting that challenge, Maria just kept pressing forward to fulfill her call — and the Holy Spirit honored her obedience.

In the middle of it all, God started visiting Maria with the gifts of the Spirit. This woman of God had one Hero — Jesus Christ. Since she was a young girl, she had wanted to do what He did. So she studied Jesus' life and copied Him. And Maria came to expect healings and miracles because she had come to intimately know the One who restored lives to wholeness wherever He went.[10]

SIGNS, WONDERS, MIRACLES!

Mother Etter later wrote of her staunch belief in the miraculous power of God. These words, penned from Maria Woodworth-Etter's own heart, powerfully articulate Heaven's purpose for this great healing mantle she carried:

> At the time of Pentecost, the one hundred and twenty came together, forsaking everything, and tarried in earnest prayer and consecration for ten days, waiting for the enduement of power to fit them for life's service. And they didn't wait in vain, for while they were yet praying the Holy Ghost came

---

[9] "Grandmother of the Pentecostal Movement," healingandrevival.com.
[10] Liardon, *Maria Woodworth-Etter*, p. 7.

upon them in wondrous power, the city was shaken, and three thousand souls were converted in a single day.

If we were ready to meet God's conditions, we would have the same results and a mighty revival would break out that would shake the world and thousands of souls would be saved. The displays of God's power on the Day of Pentecost were only a sample of what God designed should follow all through the ages. Instead of looking back to Pentecost, let us always be expecting it to come, especially in these last days. God help us to get into line and come together as one man.[11]

Whatever daunting challenge she was given or however weary she felt in meeting that challenge, Maria just kept pressing forward to fulfill her call — and the Holy Spirit honored her obedience.

Maria's ministry also became known for an unusual yet scriptural phenomenon: She had a special impartation in the realm of trances.

Trances are scriptural; they are in the Bible. It's another way that God talks to His people in a visionary form. One day when Peter went on the rooftop to pray, he fell into a trance and saw the sheet filled with "unclean" animals come down. During that trance, the Spirit of God spoke to him, and the result was Peter receiving a new revelation that would impact the entire Body of Christ: *What God has called clean, let no man call unclean* (*see* Acts 10:9-16).

---

[11] Ibid., p. 63.

This spiritual phenomenon called a trance happened a lot in Maria's meetings. Christians and non-Christians, men and women, young and old, would just be sitting in the meetings, and the power of God would hit them, causing their bodies to fall under the power or "freeze" in place while their spirit man would see and hear things in the Spirit.

When this particular demonstration of God's power first began to take place in Maria's meetings, the Holy Spirit took her back to her vision at age 13 where she stood in a field with sheaves of wheat surrounding her, and suddenly the sheaves began to fall over.

Maria later wrote of her first reactions to this unusual manifestation:

While the fear of God was on the people and I was looking on, not knowing what to do, the Spirit of God brought before me the vision I had before I started out in the work of the Lord, and said: "Don't you remember when you were carried away and saw the field of wheat and the sheaves falling? The large field of wheat was the multitudes of people you are to preach the Gospel to; the falling sheaves is what you see here tonight, the slaying power of God. This is My power; I told you I would be with you and fight your battles; it is not the wisdom of men, but the power and wisdom of God that is needed to bring sinners from darkness to light."

The Lord revealed wonderful things to me in a few moments: my fears were all gone. Those who were lying over the house as dead, after lying about two hours, all, one after another, sprang to their feet as quick as a flash, with shining faces, and shouted all over the house. I never had seen such bright conversions nor such shouting. They seemed as light as a feather. The ministers and old saints wept and praised the Lord with a loud voice. They said it was the Pentecost power; that the

Lord was visiting them in great mercy and power, and there was great victory coming.[12]

So the vision of the falling sheaves had been a "heads up" from Heaven concerning a spiritual phenomenon that would help define young Maria's future ministry. She was being prepared for the glory that was to come as she began to pursue God's call on her life.

The Power of Private Prayer
and Apostolic Preaching

Along with persistent, fearless apostolic preaching, Maria mastered another art that brought success: the art of waiting on God. This included her private prayer life, as well as waiting on God publicly for the atmosphere to be ripe.

Only He knows the private time in prayer that Maria must have spent each night preparing the spiritual atmosphere, added to the Holy Ghost singing and preaching in each evening service. The result was a *powerful* spiritual plow — a key element of this healing mantle — that broke up the hard ground of a region's spiritual atmosphere and prepared people's hearts to receive what they needed.

Along with persistent, fearless apostolic preaching, Maria mastered another art that brought success: the art of waiting on God.

---

[12] Maria Woodworth-Etter, *Signs and Wonders* (Whitaker House. Kindle Edition), p. 25.

How long it takes to break into an atmosphere depends on the principality that reigns there in the spirit realm and the amount of time it has had to shape the people under its influence into its image. But, praise God, nothing can stand up to the pressure of prayer, faith, persistence, and God's presence! Maria knew this and worked faithfully to see God's purpose manifested in each territory.

Apostolic preaching was the tool that Maria Woodworth-Etter used in these hard territories. Preaching tears down strongholds of old thought patterns that imprison man. When those thoughts are challenged, there is usually a defense mechanism of pride that stands up first to resist. That's why God told the prophets of old not to be moved by the people's faces when delivering the word of the Lord (*see* Jer. 1:17). Region after region, year after year, Maria Woodworth-Etter faithfully kept plowing and obeying that divine admonition.

In the end, Maria Woodworth-Etter started more churches than all the other ministers in the ministerial organization put together. However, Maria never really got over her sense of weakness. She didn't ever suddenly feel that she had it within her to do what God was asking. If anything, Maria came to terms with her weakness. One day she simply decided within herself that if God knew her and her weakness and still persisted in making this demand, then He would have to do something to qualify her. And that's what He did.

HOLY GHOST FIRE AND POWER

Maria asked God to give her the power He gave His disciples. He met her childlike faith with what she'd call "liquid fire," and she'd speak of the presence of angels all around. This would be the qualifying moment that Maria felt she needed, where what was lacking would be made up for by God.[13]

God's impact through Maria Woodworth-Etter in the nation always made a difference, not only for the hundreds of lost souls she would continue to reach but also in the lives of her contemporaries of the day and ministers who would be considered her junior. This group of younger ministers included some generals in the making, such as John G. Lake and Smith Wigglesworth, who were developing in their own callings and gifts. Maria was a powerful influence on these younger ministers, and they lovingly referred to her as "Mother Etter."[14]

There was rarely anyone indifferent to Maria, and I'm sure she learned to be comfortable with being misunderstood, as any true apostle must. The devil fought this mantle from the outset, and over the years, Maria endured great opposition and misunderstanding from a variety of sources — religion, the secular media, and even law enforcement. Twice she was even jailed for healing without a license!

But the Lord gave Maria a husband named Samuel Etter in her latter years to walk with her as a cherished companion and confidant. The couple was married in 1902, and Samuel proved to be a great comfort and strength to Maria in the midst of the many challenges that faced them in this pioneering ministry. He was a beloved and faithful partner in marriage and ministry until his death in 1914.

---

[13] Liardon, *Maria Woodworth-Etter*, p. 16.

[14] Roberts Liardon, *Maria Woodworth-Etter: A God's Generals Resource* (Tulsa OK: Harrison House Publishers), p. 28, Kindle Edition.

PIONEERING A HOLY GHOST HUB

Over the long decades of ministry, Maria Woodworth-Etter became known worldwide as a traveling evangelist and apostle to major U.S. cities. In her latter years, she would lay down the foundation for many upcoming denominations with her final pioneering work of planting a church. Mother Etter was able to transition successfully to this new season of ministry, putting down roots in one location to create a hub where people could come for what they needed and then go out, armed with the strength and inspiration to do what God had called them to do.

God led Mother Etter to Indianapolis, Indiana, a central location to the nation, to build the Etter Tabernacle. Some called it their home church while others came to visit the Tabernacle that housed the same power that had defined her tent ministry over the years.

Sadly, Indianapolis was also the site of tragedy for Mother Etter — the city where she lost her last living child when her daughter Lizzie was fatally injured in a trolley car accident and died at age 60. Mother Etter bravely presided over her daughter's funeral with the same steady faith with which she had faced every challenge in life through the long years of ministry.

As Mother Etter neared the end of her life, she would spend most of the week in her home, resting in bed. But on Sunday morning, some of the ladies of the church would go early to Mother Etter's house. They would dress her, put her in a chair, walk that chair out the back door of her house into the church across the alley, and set her on the stage.

The church service would start, and the congregation would sing until the anointing hit Mother Etter. When that happened, she'd stand up and start preaching like a young woman! When the service was over, she'd collapse in the chair, and the women would carry her back to her bed, where she would rest until the next church service. That's how Mother Etter lived the last couple of years of her life.

I like that part of Mother Etter's story! The anointing fixes old, cranky bodies!

**Mother Etter was able to transition successfully
to this new season of ministry,
putting down roots in one location
to create a hub where people could come
for what they needed and then go out,
armed with the strength and inspiration
to do what God had called them to do.**

Actually, I love *all* of Mother Etter's story. This was the nature of the powerful national healing mantle that entered this nation through the ground-breaking ministry of Maria Woodworth-Etter. And when Mother Etter graduated to Heaven in 1924 at age 80, buried in her signature white dress, that mantle then became available for the one who would inherit it. This is where our generational "tour" takes us next — to the life and ministry of Mother Etter's successor, Aimee Semple MacPherson.

Chapter 15

AMERICA'S TOP HEALING MANTLE 2ND GENERATION: AIMEE SEMPLE MCPHERSON

For many weeks, the Tulsa saints were praying definitely for the coming revival. Days of fasting and prayer were observed. With such prayers it was no wonder the Lord brought us through in safety [driving the "Gospel Car" to minister across the nation], no wonder the [1918 Spanish flu pandemic] ban was lifted according to the promise God gave me...no wonder sick were healed and some were raised up from death's door, no wonder our tired bodies were rested and refreshed so that we could keep going day and night with scarcely a moment to ourselves. Why, it was as though we had come in contact with a live wire, the faith and hunger and prayers of these dear people....

The epidemic still raging, and many having been weakened and afflicted, we stood hours at a time praying for the sick, and Jesus helped those who came to Him. Praise

His name! One man, crippled with rheumatism, insomuch that he could not move without acute pain, walked, ran, danced, and finally danced and leaped, perfectly healed. A man with severe stomach trouble and a sister with running sores and internal troubles were healed.... We were called into houses where poor people were lying so low, their eyes seemed glassy and the rattle in their throats, but the Lord marvelously raised them up. Bless His name![15]

BORN TO BE A SPIRITUAL PIONEER

Aimee Semple McPherson has often been described as a woman born before her time. She was truly a spiritual pioneer who paved the way in so many ways for how the Church operates and demonstrates the power of the Holy Spirit in this modern day.

Aimee was a woman who defied all odds from the day she was baptized in the Holy Spirit and throughout her life in God. To her, a challenge was fair game to be taken and conquered, and time and time again Aimee displayed her ability to rise above every obstacle and take new territory both in innovation and in demonstration of the Holy Spirit's power to heal and deliver.

Aimee was born in Canada on October 9, 1890, in the midst of controversy. Her father, a 50-year-old widower, had married 15-year-old Minnie, the young woman who had nursed his ailing wife until death.

---

[15] Aimee Semple McPherson, *This Is That: The Experiences, Sermons and Writings of Aimee Semple McPherson* (Happy Joliver Publishing. Kindle Edition), pp. 188-89.

Before taking that position as an aide to the dying woman, Minnie had been a zealous laborer for the Salvation Army. The day after her marriage, Minnie pled with the Lord to forgive her for failing to answer her call to ministry; then she asked Him to grant her a baby girl who would grow up to live the life she should have lived in His service. Soon after, Minnie became pregnant, and she never doubted that she would give birth to a little daughter in answer to her fervent prayer.

**Aimee was a woman who defied all odds
from the day she was baptized in the Holy Spirit
and throughout her life in God.**

FIRST TASTE
OF THE FIRES OF PENTECOST!

Aimee grew up in the world of the Salvation Army, where her mother served for years as an officer. Then as a young teenage girl, Aimee attended a Pentecostal revival meeting at a time when the fires of Pentecost were spreading around the nation and the world.

Aimee had heard that there were holy-roller people in town. A group of young Pentecostals had come to hold a revival meeting in her Canadian town. The rumors about this group were spreading throughout the local area: "They breathe fire, and they roll on the ground! Don't go to their meetings."

But many of the curious went to see the fire and the rolling, and Aimee was one of those who attended a meeting one night. She was actually on her way to a party at one of her friends' homes, and she thought, *I want to go see the fire-breathers. I don't understand this rolling thing, but I'd like to see it.*

So Aimee came in late and sat at the back — and from there, she witnessed people receiving the raw, volcanic Pentecostal experience of the Holy Ghost!

That's the way it was in the early days of the Pentecostal Movement. They had the volcanic early Pentecostal experience of tongues instead of the modern, milder "Charismatic experience." So you can imagine the way that many of the Methodists and Presbyterians perceived these noisy, upstart Pentecostals. Not a few of them likely thought, *These people are of the devil!*

Aimee went to the meeting looking for fire. She didn't see literal fire, but she heard strange words and saw some "holy rolling" as people fell to the ground under the power of God. So she went back the next night, drawn by the fire of Pentecost.

But that wasn't the only thing Aimee was drawn to — there was also the handsome Pentecostal evangelist, Robert Semple. He was the one preaching down the Holy Ghost fire at these Pentecostal services.

A PRECIOUS GAIN, A TRAGIC LOSS

Robert was a young Salvation Army preacher who had gotten baptized in the Holy Ghost and fire and spoke in tongues. To make a long story short, Aimee married Robert Semple, and they were the right couple. Robert loved Aimee, and they both loved the evangelistic field. Aimee's Bible school training was gained by her husband teaching her the Bible, and together they set out to save Canada and all of America.

You can always tell the highly committed — they're after the *all*. Listen to the language. "We may see a few people saved at the meeting." The person who says that won't last long in ministry. The word *all* is a God word. "I want to see *everybody* saved and Spirit-filled!" Now, *that's* revival talk! And that was how Robert and Aimee Semple spoke.

The Semples ministered for a time in Canada and in the Chicago area, but then they felt called to go to China as missionaries. So they told all of their friends in America good-bye, got on a boat, and headed out from New York to travel around the world to their destination.

**You can always tell the highly committed —
they're after the *all*. Listen to the language.
"I want to *see everybody* saved and Spirit-filled!"
Now, *that's* revival talk!**

On their way, they stopped in Ireland, Robert's home country, to visit his family and to minister wherever there was opportunity. It was in Belfast that Aimee preached the first sermon of her life. Trying to explain the strong anointing that she sensed as she preached that first time, Aimee said that her first experience preaching was like speaking in tongues, but it came out in English. And after she had preached her first sermon, she never let go of that preaching fire.

The Semples traveled on to China but soon encountered great difficulty when both of them contracted malaria. Aimee, pregnant with their child, recovered from the sickness, but Robert did not.

Aimee was faced with the unthinkable prospect of burying her young husband in China and returning with her newborn baby to her parents' home in Canada. Her mother even had to raise money in Canada to buy Aimee's boat fare. We can only imagine the deep sadness Aimee must have felt as the boat pulled away from the shores of that distant land.

'PREACH FOR ME'

Aimee returned to Canada with the thought, *I can't preach. I don't have a husband now, and I have a baby to take care of.*

But the Lord kept speaking to Aimee's heart: *"Preach for Me, Aimee. Preach for Me…"* She couldn't escape that inward voice. Yet how strong tradition can be in holding back a person from obeying the Lord!

Every day God kept speaking to Aimee: *"Preach for Me."*

"I can't, Lord. I'm a woman."

"Preach for Me."

"I can't! I don't have a husband."

As if God didn't know! He knew Aimee was a woman. He knew that Robert was in Heaven. And He knew that He was well able to help Aimee fulfill her call!

The Lord kept speaking to Aimee's heart:
"Preach for Me, Aimee. Preach for Me…"
She couldn't escape that inward voice.
Yet how strong tradition can be in holding back
a person from obeying the Lord!

Yet Aimee's tradition kept screaming back loudly at the voice of God. She was facing the same internal war that Maria Woodworth-Etter faced a generation earlier. Both were young women sensing a strong call to the ministry. Both lived in a religious world that strongly resisted the concept that a woman preacher might be God's idea. But when Aimee finally said yes and yielded to the call of God, a new anointing came upon her life.

Nobody knew young Aimee Semple's name. She wasn't famous, but she was called. She was enthusiastic. She was determined. She was committed. And she loved believing for the impossible!

So Aimee rented a little auditorium, and nobody came to the meeting. But that didn't bother Aimee. At noontime, she walked down to the middle of the square just in time for the lunch whistle to blow. Then as she stood in the middle of the city square, she stared up into the sky.

People walking by would ask, "What are you looking at, woman?" But Aimee wouldn't say a word; she'd just keep looking up. Soon in her peripheral vision, she'd know when 50 to

100 people had gathered around her. Then she'd call out, "Follow me, and I'll tell you what I'm looking for!"

**Nobody knew young Aimee Semple's name.
She wasn't famous, but she was called.
She was enthusiastic. She was determined.
She was committed. And she loved
believing for the impossible!**

At that, Aimee would take off running down the street to the door of her meeting. And when the curious crowd entered the auditorium, she'd grab her tambourine, jump up on the platform, and proclaim, "I'm looking for the King! Are you ready to meet Him yourself?" And with that, Aimee Semple would start her service!

So if Aimee didn't have a crowd already "pre-made," she'd just go out and create a crowd herself! And as she went out preaching, miracles began to follow the preaching of the Word. Her crowds began to swell into the hundreds.

A MARRIAGE
THAT DOESN'T FIT THE CALL

Then in 1912, Aimee married again — which is a good thing, *if* it's the right person. She married a man named Harold McPherson, who was a good man but *not* the right man for a woman called to a powerful ministry like Aimee Semple.

Harold didn't like anything about the concept of living by faith. When he married Aimee, his dream in life was to have a nice, "traditional American" kind of lifestyle. His idea was to marry a cute little wife who would keep the home tidy. They would have little babies who were fun to play with when he came home. He'd go to work; the kids would go to school; and the wife would stay home and cook dinner.

My question to Harold would have been, "Have you ever thought about the woman you're kissing? The one you want to marry has already ministered in Canada and America, sailed across the world, buried a husband, sailed back, and started over in ministry — and you want her to stay home and bake chicken? She isn't a 'baked chicken' kind of lady. She's the kind of woman who lays hold of demonic powers over cities and wrings their necks like *they* were chickens!"

"But I want to live in New York with my wife in my nice house." Well, then, Harold, you should have found a wife who wanted that as well.

Aimee was never going to be happy staying home and baking chicken. Harold may have wanted a stable little American life, but he had married a called woman of God whose heart burned to launch out into the unknown and preach the Gospel to the crowds while living by faith.

In 1913, a son named Rolf was born to the McPhersons. Two years later in 1915, Aimee became very ill with appendicitis. As she hovered near death, she heard a Voice ask, *"Now will you go?"* Aimee knew it was the Lord, and in that moment, she yielded and said yes once and for all. Immediately she began to improve. It was time to answer the call.

Harold may have wanted a stable little American life,
but he had married a called woman of God
whose heart burned to launch out into the unknown
and preach the Gospel to the crowds
while living by faith.

Once recovered, Aimee left her home to resume her evangelistic ministry, preaching the Gospel wherever she went and seeing miracles follow her preaching of the Word. For the first part of this fruitful season of ministry, Aimee left young Roberta in the care of her mother Minnie in Canada.[16]

A few weeks after Aimee embarked on her evangelistic travels, she wrote her husband, asking him to join her. And Harold did come to Aimee — at first, with the intention of fetching his wife back. But when he heard Aimee preach and saw the powerful fruit of her ministry, Harold decided to stay and try to help. Aimee and her husband and young son spent that first winter of 1916-1917 traveling the Eastern seaboard, their needs supplied by faith, stopping to hold powerful meetings wherever the Holy Spirit led.[17] And in every meeting, the Holy Spirit's power was in operation through this fiery woman preacher to save, heal, and set free.

This arrangement lasted for a while, but ultimately Harold decided to return to the life he was familiar with. He wasn't

---

[16] Daniel Mark Epstein, *The Life of Aimee Semple McPherson* (New York: Houghton Mifflin Harcourt Publishing Co., Kindle Edition, 1993), p. 95.
[17] Ibid., pp. 96, 114.

mean; he just said, "I can't do this." He wanted a "normal" life where he worked to make a living and came home to a wife and kids and a hot supper waiting — and that just would never be Aimee. So Harold decided to divorce Aimee, claiming abandonment.

It was a devastating blow for this young woman preacher. She reached out to her mom Minnie in Canada, who immediately prepared to travel with young Roberta to join Aimee and help her in ministry.

Aimee would tell the story something like this: "I woke up one morning, and my husband had left and was divorcing me. I had two small ones, and I didn't know if Jesus still wanted me to preach. I wasn't sure that the call was still granted to me. I went to the garden and prayed, and I heard Jesus say, *'I've never stopped loving you, and your call is intact.'* So I packed my bags and my babies' bags, got in the car, and set out to save America."

UNSTOPPABLE AIMEE

Aimee was truly an unstoppable force for God. She began traveling up and down the East Coast, preaching in her Gospel tent with signs and wonders following and drawing great crowds of people with hungry hearts. For the next seven years, Aimee would cross the United States multiple times, preaching in more than 100 cities in meetings that could last from two days to one month.

In those early years, Aimee began to primarily wear white. This practice began in 1918 while she was shopping for a new dress and the Holy Spirit spoke to her heart: *"You are a servant of all, are you not? Go upstairs and ask to see the servants' dresses."*

Aimee obeyed and bought two white servants' dresses for five dollars — which was also what she could afford at the time!

From then on, Aimee was known for most often wearing a servant's white dress and a dark cape. And years later at the end of her life, Aimee would be buried in white, just as Mother Etter had been buried in white a generation earlier.

It was in 1918 that Aimee became the first woman to travel across the nation in a car as she traversed this nation in her "Gospel Car," preaching the Gospel with her children, her mother, and an assistant.

These were days when the cars had canvas tops and the roads were dirt. You can only imagine the adventures that Aimee had to navigate as she and her little group experienced a variety of challenges — thunderstorms, muddy roads, flat tires, naysayers, etc. — along the way. And, notably, this historic ministry trip was taken during the Spanish flu pandemic!

But Aimee was up for every challenge. And even though plans had to be adjusted at times, no obstacle ever stopped Aimee or even slowed her down in her passion to win souls to Jesus and to get them healed and baptized in the Holy Ghost.

During this transcontinental ministry trip, Aimee was able to satisfy a burning desire she'd had for years to meet Mother Etter and to experience her ministry firsthand. That dream was realized when they stopped in Indianapolis to attend Mother Etter's service at Etter Tabernacle.

A quarantine had been imposed on Indianapolis when they arrived in the city because of the Spanish flu outbreak. People told her before she had left on her cross-country ministry trip, "You'll not get into Mother Etter's meeting. Indianapolis has been quarantined for weeks because this flu is spreading, and they don't want it to spread around the state."

But Aimee replied, "When I get to the border, they'll lift the quarantine!" And just an hour before she arrived in Indianapolis, the state authorities lifted the ban!

Aimee was able to drive right on into town and attend the Etter Tabernacle service that night for a midweek service. She heard Mother Etter preach and then was able to spend the next day with her and receive her blessing. And I believe within that blessing Aimee picked up an impartation as the one who would one day inherit the great healing mantle that was on Mother Etter.

**Even though plans had to be adjusted at times,
no obstacle ever stopped Aimee or even slowed her down
in her passion to win souls to Jesus and to get them
healed and baptized in the Holy Ghost.**

AMERICA'S FIRST PENTECOSTAL 'MEGACHURCH' —
FILLED WITH GOD'S GLORY

In the years that followed, Aimee seemed to draw from the influence of Maria Woodworth-Etter's ministry and to follow a rough blueprint of Mother Etter's church when pioneering her own church, the Great Angelus Temple in Los Angeles, which was later completed in 1923.

Angelus Temple would become America's first Pentecostal "megachurch," seating 5,400 people, which Aimee would fill five times on a Sunday! When the church first opened, Aimee held 21 services a week and preached in them all for the first seven weeks until she became too tired to continue and had to get some help. In the first six months of her church, there were 8,000 conversions recorded, and Aimee herself water-baptized approximately 5,000 people.

During the 1920s when the population of Los Angeles was 250,000, Aimee had more than 25,000 members in her church. That means *one-tenth* of the Los Angeles population of that time counted themselves as members of Angelus Temple! And the church is still prospering and operating to this day.

Angelus Temple would become America's first Pentecostal "megachurch," seating 5,400 people, which Aimee would fill five times on a Sunday!

In 1924, Aimee also became a media pioneer when she started the first Christian radio station in all of America. It was only the third radio station in Los Angeles, and the station continues to operate to the present day.

Aimee would call for what she called "ambulance days" at Angelus Temple. It's a historical fact in Los Angeles history that whenever she did that, the ambulances from LA to San Diego would get booked by the hundreds, until hospitals had to fight to keep some ambulances for actual emergencies!

The ambulances would line up in front of her church — a long line that continued around the block. Aimee would stand there and pray for the occupant of an ambulance; then that ambulance would drive off and the next ambulance would move up for its turn. Aimee would keep this up for an entire day, and miraculous testimonies would abound to God's glory!

Aimee also called for "stretcher days" in the Temple. These were healing services set aside exclusively for those who were incapacitated and couldn't be a part of the regular prayer lines. Aimee would set aside an afternoon and announce, "I will be praying only for those who have to attend on stretchers." Again and again, she'd pray as she grasped the hand of a patient lying on a stretcher, and then she'd help the person stand up — healed!

So many great miracles happened in the course of Aimee's healing ministry in Angelus Temple, but I will relate just one as an example. Someone who attended the Temple brought a blind man to church who had no pupils, just the whites of his eyes. Aimee turned this person around so the entire congregation of 5,400 people could see the miracle that was about to take place; then she said, "I want you to watch Jesus give eyes to this blind man."

Aimee said a simple prayer: "Jesus, we need some eyes. Could You help us?"

Those sitting near the platform said they saw little swirls begin to move in the whites of the man's eyes. Then in an instant, God did a creative miracle in front of 5,400 people. The man had two new eyes and could see perfectly! Yet that was just a typical service at Angelus Temple with Aimee Semple McPherson!

Aimee also called for "stretcher days" in the Temple.
Again and again, she'd pray as she grasped
the hand of a patient lying on a stretcher,
and then she'd help the person stand up — healed!

OUTSHINING HOLLYWOOD
WHILE PREACHING JESUS

The roaring '20s was the golden era of Hollywood and Los Angeles, and Aimee was bigger than all the stars. Hollywood offered her three different contracts to be in the movies over the years. Film producers knew that such a movie would be guaranteed to be highly profitable because Aimee was in it.

But Aimee declined every offer that came her way from Hollywood. "I shine only for One, and that is Christ," she'd respond. She didn't take any of those offers.

Meanwhile, Aimee outshone Hollywood in the field of drama on the stage of her own church! Even members of the Hollywood elite would come to Aimee's church to see her illustrated sermons on Sunday nights. She'd decorate the stage, dress herself up to fit a part, and include other actors to help tell the story. One Sunday evening she was going to preach about

Jonah and the big whale, so she walked out of the mouth of a huge "whale" prop and started preaching!

Another Sunday night Aimee was honoring the city's policemen, and they had turned out in force to her church. Dressed up as a policewoman, she drove up a ramp on a motorcycle and onto the stage, blew her whistle, and shouted, "Stop! You're all going to hell." Then she commenced preaching the Gospel to the policemen, employing the anointing on her life, her love for people, and her "think outside the box" kind of creativity to get those policemen saved. That was Sister Aimee!

KIDNAPPED — *TWICE*

As dramatic as Aimee was in her style of preaching, nothing compared to the actual drama that occurred in real life during the course of her ministry. And of all the dramatic events Aimee experienced, nothing surpassed the fact that she was actually kidnapped twice, and the first time it was by the Klu Klux Klan![18]

The first instance happened in 1922 as Aimee was ministering at a public hall in Denver, Colorado. After the service, she was being interviewed by a woman reporter when she received a request to come outside and pray for an invalid. She took the reporter with her to witness the prayer — but when they stepped outside, they were suddenly blindfolded, abducted, and driven to a private KKK meeting! It turned out that the Klan members wanted their own private sermon preached by the famous woman preacher, Mrs. McPherson.

---

[18] Epstein, pp. 241-43.

You'd think Aimee McPherson's would be afraid to preach to this bunch of hooded KKK members. But Aimee's attitude was, *Well, I have them all in one place, so let's get them for Jesus!* So she started preaching like she would at a Gospel crusade, and that night there were Klan members burning their hoods instead of crosses! One Klan member who was in that meeting later even became an elder in her church!

As dramatic as Aimee was in her style of preaching, nothing compared to the actual drama that occurred in real life during the course of her ministry.

Afterward, the two women were blindfolded and taken back to the hall in Denver. The reporter published a riveting story about the kidnapping that increased Aimee's popularity and brought in more money for the building of the Angelus Temple.

The second kidnapping became as famous in the American culture of that time as was the O.J. Simpson trial in our lifetime. It occurred in 1926, and it became the greatest controversy and scandal of Aimee's ministry.

On May 18, Aimee was enjoying an afternoon on the beach with her secretary. After making some final notes on her next sermon, she asked her secretary to go call in the changes to the staff at Angelus Temple. When the secretary returned to the beach, Aimee had vanished. Thinking Aimee had gone for a swim, the secretary scanned the waters. When no trace could be found of Aimee, she called the authorities.

Over the next 32 days, Aimee's disappearance became the hottest news story in the world. Los Angeles beaches were combed, and outlying waters were searched, but nothing was found. A couple of ransom notes were received at Angelus Temple and discarded as phony by Minnie, Aimee's mother. Aimee sightings from coast to coast abounded.

Three days after her memorial service was finally held on June 20, Aimee walked into Douglas, Arizona, from the desert at Agua Prieta, Mexico. When asked, she explained who she was.

Over the next 32 days, Aimee's disappearance became the hottest news story in the world. Aimee sightings from coast to coast abounded.

Aimee later explained what had happened to her that day on the beach. She had been deceived by a man who had walked up to her and said, "My little baby is dying, and my wife is in the car holding him. Would you come over and pray for our child?"

But when Aimee walked over to the car and bent down to say hello to the woman, the man shoved Aimee in the back seat and the woman put a cloth soaked in chloroform over her face to knock her out. When Aimee woke up, she was being held captive in an isolated shack in the desert. It turns out they had driven Aimee across the Arizona border into Mexico, where they held her captive while trying to obtain ransom money.

The captors sent a kidnapping note, and then later a second follow-up note, each demanding $500,000 to return Aimee.[19] But when Minnie was given the notes, she thought they were hoaxes carried out by conmen trying to cash in on the crisis. So Minnie dismissed the notes as frauds, not realizing they were legitimate.

Weeks later, Aimee found a way to cut through her bonds and escape while the woman guarding her was away buying goods. Aimee walked through the desert for hours until finally reaching the outskirts of a little town called Douglas, Arizona. She knocked on the door of the first little house, but no one answered. She walked on to the next little house and collapsed on the front porch.

The man who lived there opened his door, startled by the sight of an unconscious woman lying on his porch. He took her to the little local hospital and called the chief of police while the medical staff worked to revive her.

Eventually Aimee came to, and there sat the Douglas police chief. "Who are you?"

"I'm Aimee Semple McPherson."

"No, she's dead."

"No, I'm Aimee Semple McPherson" — and the two started arguing.

Aimee said, "Pick up the phone and call this number," giving the officer the phone number of her home in Los Angeles. Her mother answered the phone, and the police chief said, "I

---

[19] Raymond L. Cox, *The Verdict Is In* (Los Angeles: Research Publishers, 1983), pp. 41, 56.

have a woman here who says she's Aimee Semple McPherson. Will you talk to her?"

Her mother retorted, "No, I will not! Why don't you people leave me alone? You reporters tortured her, and you torture me!"

The chief of police answered, "Hey, please just talk to her, and then you can tell me what to believe."

Minnie finally agreed, and the officer handed the phone to Aimee as she lay in the hospital bed. Aimee told her mother a family secret that only the family would know. Minnie knew then: *Aimee was alive!*

The church rented a small plane to fly to Douglas, Arizona. The goal was to get to Aimee as soon as possible and then bring her home via train. Aimee's young son Rolf was aboard with the crew for that flight, along with his grandmother and sister. He recalled to me later that they weren't alone on that trip. They could look out the window of the plane and see about 100 other small planes heading in the same direction! All were afraid that if they didn't arrive there and land first — whether at the small local airport or on the nearby fields — they'd never get on the ground, because everyone was coming to see the same thing: Aimee — *alive*. It was almost as exciting as Jesus being raised from the dead!

Approximately 50,000 people gathered to welcome Aimee back to Angelus Temple.[20] It was an occasion of great rejoicing for all who loved Aimee — but her ordeal had just begun.

---

[20] Cox, *The Verdict Is In*, p. 96.

THE DIFFICULT YEARS

Although Aimee's claim of kidnapping would never vary over time, her story would be skewered in the press as many questioned its truth. No kidnappers were ever identified or apprehended; however, it should be noted that Aimee had made many enemies in the underworld of Los Angeles. She had gotten several key people in that world saved and allowed their testimonies, which exposed the criminal deeds of their former associates, to be aired on her radio program.

Also, Los Angeles had a "kidnapping culture" at that time. The kidnappers likely made the mistake of assuming that her prominence as the leader of a large church meant that she was rich.

The years following this scandal not only were full of controversy, but they were also difficult in other ways for Aimee. She was facing multiple lawsuits as her promoters pursued faulty business ventures and left her to deal with the fallout. In addition, Aimee's relationship with her mother and ministry administrator, Minnie, was deteriorating.

Minnie kept crossing back and forth between opposite roles. Sometimes she was the devoted helper, gifted at organization and administration, and other times she was a critical, controlling overseer of a ministry that she didn't understand. It finally came to the point in 1927 that Aimee, with the agreement of her Board of Elders, dismissed her mother from her position.

During this difficult time period, it seemed to Aimee that everyone who had ever been close to her was either betraying her or withering under the weight of the criticism coming from all sides. The strain of all the upheaval over these tumultuous years finally caused her to suffer an emotional and physical breakdown in 1930.

For ten months, Aimee was confined to a Malibu beach cottage under a physician's constant care. When she came out of that time of seclusion, she was in a lonely and vulnerable position. The price of fame was high, leaving her with no close friends and craving companionship.

A THIRD MARRIAGE — A WRONG TURN

It was in that emotional state that Aimee married a third time in 1931. This time her chosen mate was a big, plus-size man named David Hutton. In Aimee's desperate need for love and protection, she had built a lofty image of this man in her imagination that simply wasn't true.

Hutton had played in the honky-tonks and bars of southern California and was actually a playboy who liked going out with many women. It would later be learned that he had accepted a dare presented to him by his friends: "See if you can get Aimee to marry you."

Accepting the dare, David Hutton got a job as the Angelus Temple worship leader and started working his charms on Aimee. Soon they got married, but it wasn't long before Hutton began to show his true colors. Behind closed doors, Hutton started slapping, pushing, and cursing Aimee — and then he divorced her.

The day that news of the divorce hit the newspapers, Aimee had to go teach Bible school class. She walked into that class with more than 1,000 students in it and tried to teach her lesson, acting like everything was fine. But it wasn't long before Aimee broke down and began to cry in the middle of her class.

**In Aimee's desperate need for love and protection,
she had built a lofty image of this man
in her imagination that simply wasn't true.**

The students rushed the little platform to comfort Sister Aimee — praying for her, loving on her, speaking encouraging words over her. But it seems there is always one person who does something he or she shouldn't do in a sensitive situation like that. That one person spoke up and asked Aimee: "Why did you marry him?"

Great question — wrong timing. Nevertheless, Aimee was willing to answer the question. She said, "I was lonely, and I thought it was love. I made a mistake."

Being a gift to the Body of Christ and carrying a mantle doesn't negate the humanity of a person's life. As ministers must manage their faith, they must also manage their lives.

BUILDING A LEGACY
TO IMPACT FUTURE GENERATIONS FOR JESUS

People called Aimee "the much-married evangelist" — married three times, divorced twice. She would continue on in ministry, making news through the Depression and the war years with her ground-breaking methods to help hurting humanity and win souls for Christ. During these years, Aimee multiplied her reach exponentially through the planting of hundreds of affiliate churches.

**Being a gift to the Body of Christ and
carrying a mantle doesn't negate the humanity
of a person's life. As ministers must manage their faith,
they must also manage their lives.**

But Aimee was getting older, and her body was beginning to weaken, in part from the fast pace she had kept during her years of ministry. In addition, throughout the latter 1920s and the 1930s, Aimee had also faced the stress of ongoing conflicts and legal challenges that impacted the ministry. One such conflict involved her daughter Roberta, who in 1937 successfully sued her mother's lawyer for slander.

Roberta was removed from leadership that same year[21] and subsequently left the ministry, establishing a new life for herself in New York City. In the years that followed, Roberta maintained communication with her mother from a distance and still gave financially at times to help the church. However, Aimee's daughter would never return to Los Angeles to take part in leading the ministry. This was a deep disappointment for Aimee, one that she had to learn to deal with in her heart so she could keep moving forward.

---

[21] Epstein, pp. 408-411.

It was in 1944 during a ministry trip to Oakland, California, that Aimee met an untimely death from an accidental overdose of her medication. Thankfully, Aimee's faithful son Rolf stepped in to lead the ministry as an anointed administrator, and the work continued to grow. The powerful spiritual legacy Aimee left behind in the form of the Foursquare denomination she founded continues to produce mighty fruit for God's Kingdom throughout the world.

Aimee McPherson, quite unlike Mother Etter, was known to be flashy and showy — fitting in with and even surpassing in extravagance and pizzazz the Hollywood crowd. Many criticized Aimee's makeup and her theatrics, but no one could deny the innumerable souls won for Jesus throughout her life of ministry.

The powerful spiritual legacy Aimee left behind in the form of the Foursquare denomination she founded continues to produce mighty fruit for God's Kingdom throughout the world.

Aimee would become known as one of America's greatest evangelists of the early 20th century. And it was the great power show of God through healings and miracles that caused many to conclude there had been a generational transfer of the great healing mantle of Mother Etter to Aimee McPherson.[22]

---

[22] Liardon, *Maria Woodworth-Etter*, pp. 28-30, 33.

Chapter 16

America's Top Healing Mantle 3rd Generation: Kathryn Kuhlman

Miss Kuhlman's face breaks into a wide smile as she greets the vast sea of people. She flows across the stage, sharing from her heart the truth that she knows so well about the One whom she trusts beyond all human understanding. Pointing toward the main floor, she declares, "There — asthma is being healed." "I see the Holy Spirit in this area of the auditorium," she exclaims and points to the wheelchair area. Tears begin to trickle down her cheeks as she looks at the upper balcony and states, "Up there, someone is being healed of sugar diabetes."

Suddenly, it's happening all over the building! People are rising from wheelchairs and from seats, amazed and inexpressibly happy. Braces are discarded. Wheelchairs are abandoned. Hearing aids are removed — forever! They are healed! Up on stage they go, to stand in front of the woman who has summoned them, the woman who believes in miracles.[23]

No Turning Back

S oon after Aimee's death in 1944, there sat a woman at her gravesite who had known of and admired Aimee's ministry. At the time, this woman was in the worst position of her life and had gone to the gravesite of Aimee Semple McPherson to sit on one of the benches near Aimee's grave and reflect. While this woman sat there, an elderly Latino woman, with the help of her granddaughter, walked up the small hill to Aimee's grave and sat on the bench on the other side.

The grandmother began talking to her little granddaughter: "I want to introduce you to the lady who brought our family to faith in Christ. This is where she is buried..." And the grandmother went on to tell the story of how her heart was moved to come to Christ as she heard Aimee preach when she was a teenager.

The elderly woman explained to her granddaughter, "That's why your mom and dad and your uncle and aunt are Christians. That's why *you* are a Christian — because this servant of the Lord obeyed God and came to Los Angeles to preach Christ. I wanted you to know how the Gospel was brought to us."

The woman sitting on the opposite bench at the gravesite was Kathryn Kuhlman, and as she overheard this grandmother's

---

[23] Roberts Liardon, *Kathryn Kuhlman* (New Kensington, PA: Whitaker House, 2005, Kindle Edition), p. 13.

words, she wept and said to Jesus, "Before I die, I hope someone can say that about me because I helped them."

This striking scene became forever etched in my mind after being related to me by one of Kathryn's secretaries years after her death. The call of God burned within Kathryn's heart as it once had burned in Aimee's heart. However, Kathryn Kuhlman had gotten sidelined by her own wrong choice six years earlier.

Kathryn had come to Los Angeles in 1943, five years after marrying the wrong person and entering into a season of ministerial oblivion. Years earlier as a young woman traveling the West Coast in ministry with her sister and brother-in-law, Kathryn had even attended night classes for a short time at Aimee's Bible school at Angeles Temple.[24]

**The call of God burned within Kathryn's heart
as it once had burned in Aimee's heart. However,
Kathryn Kuhlman had gotten sidelined
by her own wrong choice six years earlier.**

Now sitting near Aimee's gravesite, Kathryn was at a crossroads, determined to make a decision from which there would be no turning back.

---

[24] Wayne Warner, *Kathryn Kuhlman: The Woman Behind the Miracles* (Ann Arbor: MI: Servant Publications, 1993), p. 34-35.

BRIGHT BEGINNINGS

Kathryn's ministry had begun with bright promise. Born on her family's farm near the small town of Concordia, Missouri, she was a precocious, independent-minded little girl growing up, known to love her daddy above all else. Her mom was a Methodist and her daddy was a Baptist. Both went to their separate churches every Sunday morning.

When Kathryn was 14 years old, she was standing in the back of her mother's Methodist church, and the last song of that service was being sung. But as the congregation was singing the benedictory song, the power of God came upon young Kathryn, and she began to cry and shake so much that her hymnal almost fell out of her hands.

Kathryn didn't know what to do. So she put down the hymnal, walked to the front of the church, sat down on a front pew, and began weeping. The older ladies of the church came to comfort her: "Oh, don't cry. You'll be okay." No one present discerned that Kathryn was under the convicting power of the Holy Spirit.

Yet somehow in the middle of the last moments of that service, Kathryn said yes to Jesus, and she was born again. She went home that day to tell her dad, as she had always told him everything: "Dad, Dad, something happened to me! I've been born again!"

All Kathryn's dad said was, "Well, that's nice, Kathryn." He never came to truly understand the miracle that had just taken place in his daughter.

From that day forward, Kathryn fell completely in love with Jesus. At the age of 16, she jumped at the opportunity to join her older sister Myrtle and her husband, Everett Parrott, in their itinerant ministry.

For five years, young Kathryn willingly put her hand to every chore that would help lighten the load as the three traveled around the Midwest, preaching the Gospel at every opportunity. Along the way, another young woman named Helen Gulliford was added to the team. Helen was an accomplished pianist and a great asset in helping to set the atmosphere for the Holy Spirit to move in the meetings.

THE INCEPTION
OF KATHRYN KUHLMAN'S MINISTRY

Mounting troubles in the Parrotts' marriage finally resulted in Everett traveling alone to minister in a new location, leaving Myrtle to preach at the current meetings in Boise, Idaho, with Kathryn and Helen assisting. That plan didn't go very well, because Myrtle's strength wasn't in preaching. Faced with sparse attendance at their meetings and dwindling funds, Myrtle decided to rejoin her husband.

That left Kathryn and Helen in Boise, Idaho, and Kathryn did *not* want to go back to Concordia. She had only five dollars and a big suitcase with hardly anything in it. But she prayed that night and believed that the Lord told her it was time to start her own ministry.

Kathryn and Helen accepted an invitation from a local pastor to stay in that area and hold some meetings. Kathryn preached, and Helen provided the worship music — and from the very beginning, their meetings bore fruit.

From Idaho to Utah to Colorado, over the next five years this two-woman team proved to be a powerful combination. No place was too humble to hold their meetings or to serve as their temporary lodgings. Whatever adverse situation Kathryn and Helen faced along the way, these determined ladies found a way to press through and keep moving forward. And as the two women went through every door of opportunity that presented itself to preach the Gospel, they found that God prospered their way. The power and presence of God was evident as many gave their lives to the Lord.

Kathryn preached, and Helen provided the worship music — and from the very beginning, their meetings bore fruit.

'PRAYER CHANGES THINGS' IN DENVER!

In 1933, this two-woman team traveled to Pueblo, Colorado, to hold a six-week crusade in Pueblo. While there, they added a business manager to the team, and when it was time to move on to Denver, they took a huge step of faith and rented a warehouse.

It was a God step. Immediately crowds began to fill the building to capacity every night. The response was so great that eventually Kathryn agreed to stay in Denver. By May 1935, a building had been bought and renovated, and Denver Revival Tabernacle opened with a huge neon sign over the building that shouted to the world: *"Prayer Changes Things."*

The revival center soon developed into an organized church with Sunday school and outreaches into prisons and nursing homes. Kathryn also began a radio program called, "Smiling Through." Every endeavor met with success, and thousands of people attended Kathryn's meetings over the next four years.

Kathryn Kuhlman's revival center became the church that itinerant ministers had to visit when they traveled to Colorado. All the "who's who" of visiting ministers wanted to come preach in her pulpit, including Raymond T. Richey, who held a three-week revival there.

KATHRYN 'TAKES THE BAIT'

In early 1937, Burroughs A. Waltrip was one of those visiting ministers who preached at Denver Revival Tabernacle. He had started a church in Mason City, Iowa, and was on the radio there. At the time, Rev. Waltrip was the dominant force of ministry in that part of Iowa.

Waltrip started traveling back and forth between Mason City and Denver to preach in Kathryn's church. He was a handsome man, skilled at maneuvering circumstances to benefit himself. At the time, Burroughs Waltrip was married and had two young sons, but he found this young woman pastor attractive and decided to start divorce proceedings.

Meanwhile, Burroughs told Kathryn that his wife had abandoned him and that he was divorced. Kathryn believed him, and they started dating while he was still married.

Later when Kathryn found out he was still legally married, she of course was furious. But Burroughs was ready with his explanation. He told her, "My marriage was never real before

God because I never loved her." And for some foolish reason, Kathryn Kuhlman bought the lie. She had allowed herself to fall in love with this man she affectionately called "Mister," and she wanted to believe him.

Everyone close to Kathryn tried to dissuade her from continuing down this path toward marrying this man of questionable morals. But in October 1938, Kathryn Kuhlman became Mrs. Burroughs A. Waltrip.

During the wedding ceremony, Kathryn became agitated and at one point even fainted. After the wedding, she almost immediately knew she had made a mistake and even left Burroughs at the hotel to find her friend and tell her that she wanted to get the marriage annulled. But in the end, Kathryn yielded to Burrough's persuasion and to her own love for the man and decided to try to make the best of her decision to say "yes."

**For some foolish reason, Kathryn Kuhlman
bought the lie. She had allowed herself
to fall in love with this man she affectionately called
"Mister," and she wanted to believe him.**

However, the couple soon found that both of their ministries were quickly disintegrating as a result of widespread disapproval of their marriage. Both of their churches and ministries lost their good reputation. First, the congregation of Denver Revival Tabernacle scattered; then Burroughs' work in Mason City shut down. No one invited either of them to minister anymore; no one wanted them.

The couple lost everything they had worked for, including a living income. And even when a rare ministry opportunity did arise, people wanted Kathryn, not Burroughs. Burroughs didn't like that and became jealous. He made the rule, "If I'm not preaching, she can't come." That kind of rule doesn't last long before a person loses his whole ministry.

Kathryn stayed with Burroughs for six years. Although she truly loved "Mister," these were sad, lean years for her. When she met Burroughs, she'd had a good name, a strong ministry, and a thriving church of more than 2,000 in Denver. But by 1944, the couple was living in Los Angeles, California, and as Kathryn sat on that bench near Aimee Semple McPherson's grave, she had nothing left. Her ministry opportunities had dried up, and her marriage was ending. She had just walked to a dead-end street in Los Angeles, California, and had engaged in a "valley of decision" conversation with Jesus.

'THE MOMENT KATHYRN KUHLMAN DIED'

Remembering that pivotal moment in her life, Kathryn would say, "I walked to a dead-end street in southern California. I know the spot; I know the hour; I know the moment that Kathryn Kuhlman died. But in that moment when I died, I found the greatest power of life. I looked to Jesus, and I said, 'I have nothing. I have no money. I have no name. I have nothing to give You except this: I love You with all of my heart. If You can use me, Lord, please use me.'"

At that moment, this healing mantle was looking for a new generational vessel. According to Kathryn when speaking about her ministry in later years, God had asked three other men before her, and they had said, "No, I'm too busy." "No, I don't want that." "Next year, Lord."

Kathryn Kuhlman was God's fourth choice, and at the worst moment of her life, this mantle came upon her. But from the moment Kathryn made her decision, she never wavered from answering the call of God on her life. She never deviated from the path God had set for her, and she never saw "Mister" again.

Kathryn would say, I know the spot;
I know the hour; I know the moment
that Kathryn Kuhlman died. But in that moment
when I died, I found the greatest power of life.

Kathryn got on a one-way train to Franklin, Pennsylvania, and never looked back. As it turned out, Franklin would prove to be a fruitful home base where Kathryn could feel accepted while she worked her way back fully into ministry.

The elders of a church in town with no pastor invited Kathryn Kuhlman to hold a meeting. Then on Monday morning after the Sunday meetings, the elders and their wives and Ms. Kuhlman had breakfast together before Kathryn left for her next engagement. The elders happily said to Kathryn, "We've got some good news! We found ourselves a pastor."

Oh, wonderful! Who is it?" Kathryn asked.

"You!"

"Oh, no!" Kathryn protested.

"Yes! God told us it was you."

Kathryn replied, "You don't want me as your pastor. I'm a divorced woman."

So the elders said, "Excuse us for a moment." They went out and got in a "football huddle" to talk it over. A few minutes later, they returned and said, "We're not asking the divorced Kathryn Kuhlman to be our pastor. *This* Kathryn is our pastor."

All the hurt and rejection Kathryn Kuhlman had experienced began to melt away in that moment of acceptance. Her heart had found a place to heal, working with a group of elders who refused to allow what had been forgiven from Kathryn's past to have any voice in their present.

A SEASON OF RESTORATION
AND GROWTH IN MINISTRY

Over the next two years, Kathryn would branch out to minister in some midwestern and southern states. During those early years of Kathryn's comeback, certain elements of the Church didn't treat Kathryn well. At times a pastor would ask her to preach, and then that pastor would receive a telegram or a note informing him that she was divorced. There were instances when Kathryn actually had the microphone taken from her as she was told to get off the platform and leave town.

Kathryn shed many tears in those early difficult years as the pain of what she had lost echoed in her heart and mind. She didn't talk about her loss publicly, but in the privacy of her relationship with the Lord, she dealt with knowing what she had given up: her heart desire to stay married to the man she loved and to one day raise a family.

But Kathryn loved Jesus with all her heart, and she was determined never to turn back from her decision to stay faithful to her call. She may have suffered in private, but among the people, she simply kept ministering His love wherever she could find an opportunity.

Finally, in 1946, there was a dramatic shift toward favor in Kathryn's ministry. She was invited to hold a series of meetings in the 1,500-seat Gospel Tabernacle in Franklin. From the beginning, Kathryn's meetings were so gloriously fruitful in the Tabernacle that it was almost as if the last eight years never existed.

Soon after her Tabernacle meetings commenced, Kathryn also started daily radio broadcasts in Oil City, Pennsylvania. The response was so great that she soon added a station in Pittsburgh. Instead of being shunned, Kathryn's ministry office was now being flooded with mail.

Up until this time, Kathryn had been mainly praying for people to receive salvation. But during her season at the Tabernacle, she began praying and laying hands on people who came for healing. It was soon after the end of World War II, and the Holy Spirit was working to restore the gift of healing to the Body of Christ. Having faithfully followed the leading of the Holy Spirit on the path to restoring her ministry, Kathryn found herself riding the crest of that spiritual wave.

The wildly successful Tabernacle meetings continued indefinitely past the original booking. Then in 1947, Kathryn taught a series on the Holy Spirit, saying things as she taught that were revelation even to her. From that point on, a new phenomenon began to occur in Kathryn's meetings: People began to get miraculously healed as Kathryn preached without anyone laying hands on them!

Once the testimonies of miraculous healings started multiplying, the crowds at Kathryn's meetings started growing rapidly. She held a meeting in Carnegie Hall in Pittsburgh, and every seat was filled. The same scene played out wherever she traveled to hold meetings in large halls and auditoriums.

**It was soon after the end of World War II,
and the Holy Spirit was working to restore
the gift of healing to the Body of Christ.
Having faithfully followed the leading
of the Holy Spirit on the path to restoring
her ministry, Kathryn found herself riding
the crest of that spiritual wave.**

But Kathryn's home base was still the Gospel Tabernacle in Franklin. Kathryn had a strong sense of loyalty to the people of Franklin who had been so kind to her when she was restarting her ministry. Her close associates told Kathryn that it would be wise to move her ministry headquarters into the city of Pittsburgh. She responded, "No! The roof would have to cave in before I would believe God wanted me to move to Pittsburgh!"

On Thanksgiving Day of 1950, the roof of the building where Kathryn had ministered so often caved in from the weight of the greatest snowfall on record for that area. Three weeks later, Kathryn moved to Fox Chapel, a suburb of Pittsburgh, where she lived until her death many years later.

THE HOLY SPIRIT'S POWER
THROUGH 'THE MOST ORDINARY PERSON
IN THE WORLD'

The elders of the small church in Franklin hadn't known that this Kathryn Kuhlman they were asking to be their pastor would become *the* Kathryn Kuhlman that the world would come to know. Kathryn Kuhlman was shocked as well when she became that Kathryn Kuhlman! She would say, "I know better than anyone else that I have no healing virtue or power. I cannot heal anyone; I'm the most ordinary person in the world." That was the way she viewed herself.

Kathryn would explain to congregations, "You say, 'Kathryn, touch me, touch me!' But it's not my touch that is needed; it is *His* touch that you need. For it is not some of self and some of Him; it is *none* of self and *all* of Him. He's not looking for golden vessels or silver vessels; He is looking for *yielded* vessels."

The years went by, and Kathryn's ministry grew. By the mid-1950s, it had gotten to a place in her meetings that the team would open the building hours before the service was to begin and the auditorium would quickly fill to capacity. So Kathryn put a new rule in place: "When the building is full and the fire marshal locks the door, call me; I'll come and we'll start church."

When it was time, the team would call Kathryn and say, "It's full, Ms. Kuhlman." She'd reply, "All right, I'm coming." Wearing her signature white dress, Kathryn would come to the green room to greet the VIPs who had come back to say hello to her and then graciously send them off to their seats.

Something sacred would happen as Kathryn then prepared to come out before the people. During those critical moments, everyone who worked with her behind the scenes knew exactly what they were to do and what they should not do.

Kathryn would explain to congregations, "It's not my touch that is needed; it is *His* touch that you need. For it is not some of self and some of Him; it is *none* of self and *all* of Him."

Kathryn called those moments before every service "the time when Kathryn Kuhlman dies a thousand deaths." She would pace back and forth behind the curtain or the door and pray until there was very little of Kathryn left and she was simply a yielded vessel through which the power of God could flow to eradicate disease and demonic oppression. She knew this would be some people's last hope. If they did not get touched, they were going to die.

Kathryn was also very skilled and comfortable waiting for the public sense of God's presence, a time where all hearts seemed to unite. Mother Etter referred so many times in her sermons to that place of Pentecost, where the people waited in unity and came into one accord. Then the power would come, or as the old-timers might say, "The blessing flowed."

In a Kathryn Kuhlman meeting, the congregation would sing along with the choir often for hours waiting on God. Kathryn wouldn't even come to the pulpit until the Holy Spirit was tangibly present. Often by that time, many people were simply healed in His presence, never receiving ministry from her personally.

And Kathryn knew that she couldn't do a thing on her own to help anyone. So she would pace and pray and die, as she would say — and when she felt ready, she'd walk so quickly out on the stage wearing that flowing white dress that it looked like she was floating. Then the divine electricity that we call the anointing of God would begin to manifest as people were gloriously and instantaneously healed and set free!

I was in three of her meetings and met her once as a little boy, so I have experienced this firsthand. Someone would get healed — and then boom, boom, boom! Healings started popping like popcorn all over the auditorium. The rhythm of her meetings didn't even go up and down; it just kept rising to a crescendo, lasting three, four, or sometimes five hours.

In one of Ms. Kuhlman's miracle services that I attended as a boy, I was sitting about four rows back from the wheelchair section, which covered half of the bottom floor of the auditorium. There were probably 300 to 500 wheelchairs in the section.

All of a sudden we could hear a wind begin to lightly blow. I thought it was the air conditioner coming on. *Whoooosh* — the wind hit the wheelchair section, and approximately 30 of those people suddenly jumped up and walked out of their wheelchairs! Some were instantly whole; others shuffled a little at first and then began to walk normally. Even as a young boy, the power of that experience at Ms. Kuhlman's meeting marked me for life. It ignited an undying hunger in me for the tangible anointing of the Holy Spirit that urges me on in my spiritual race to this day.

Kathryn Kuhlman walked in an unusual dimension of power. She carried a tangible touch of the Holy Spirit all the time, because she carried the mantle as a lifestyle, not as a church event.

When Kathryn came to the airport, she'd be walking to get on the plane and people would recognize her and ask her to pray for them. When she did, they would often fall to the floor from the power of the anointing. Sometimes people would be slain in the Spirit in the airport when Kathryn simply walked by them!

Kathryn Kuhlman walked in an unusual dimension of power. She carried a tangible touch of the Holy Spirit all the time, because she carried the mantle as a lifestyle, not as a church event.

In 1965, Kathryn launched her television program "I Believe in Miracles" on CBS. For the next decade, it would become the longest-running religious program in CBS history.

In the last years of Kathryn's life, preachers were not the only ones inviting her; even mayors of cities were asking her to come. Kathryn would receive invitations from city leaders that said, "Please come and hold a gospel healing crusade; we'll give you our largest auditorium."

The size of the crowds grew bigger and bigger over the years in Kathryn's meetings. And as the crowds increased, so did the outstanding miracles. It's all part of this great healing mantle for America that God placed on the earth — and I believe it's for every generation until the end of the age when Jesus returns!

Kathryn would die too soon as the result of an enlarged heart on February 21, 1976, in the ICU of St. John's Hospital in

Tulsa, Oklahoma. Later I was able to talk to the nurse in charge of taking care of Kathryn who was there in the middle of the night when she died. This nurse said that at the moment Kathryn's heart stopped, the power in the entire hospital went out. The backup generator power came on for four or five minutes, and then — *bam!* The backup power temporarily went out as well throughout the hospital!

Then all of a sudden, the aroma of roses filled three floors of the hospital. The nurse said to me, "Ms. Kuhlman had told us that afternoon, 'I love roses, and I'd like roses at my departure.'"

So Kathryn Kuhlman transitioned at the end of her life with an angelic escort that brought the aroma of roses to accompany her departure. And arriving in Heaven, she saw Jesus face to face for the very first time — the One that throughout her life, she loved most of all.

THE POWER OF A GENERATIONAL MANTLE

We've seen that this particular healing mantle has common threads that can be observed. For instance, in each generation, the reputation of this top healing mantle becomes national in scope as great crowds assemble to witness the outstanding miracles that occur on a regular basis. In each generation, the mantle carrier also made a conscious decision to primarily wear white when ministering.

There are also common ways that the enemy attacks the one who carries this mantle in each generation. It is the successor's responsibility to stay aware of Satan's strategies and take all necessary steps to guard against them.

In the case of this national healing mantle, all three generations of mantle carriers faced challenges in assuming their role as women preachers, which was frowned upon in society in their time. This was especially true for divorced women preachers, and all three eventually faced marital troubles that led to divorce.

All three also suffered the pain of loss concerning the subject of children. For Maria, she endured the grief of outliving all her children, five of whom died as young children.

Aimee went through a period of conflict with her daughter Roberta concerning the running of the ministry. Roberta was eventually removed from her leadership position as a result of a dispute concerning Aimee's lawyer and subsequently moved across the nation to start a new life in New York City. So although Aimee had her son Rolf as her faithful helper in the fulfillment of her call, she never again had Roberta by her side in ministry.

As for Kathryn, she had made the decision on that dead-end street to lay on the altar her desire for a husband and children in order to fulfill the call of God that compelled her. Only the One to whom Kathryn surrendered her life knows the inner pain that her decision caused her during her years on this earth.

In addition, the national attention that helped grow these women's ministries also became a heavy burden at times. All three generations of these mantle carriers endured opposition from multiple sources. They faced persecution from the religious, from the media, and from a secular society that didn't understand their assignment from Heaven or the God they served.

Finally, the enemy's strategies to stop this mantle from operating manifested in a similar way near the end of each woman's life. All three had heart issues that helped contribute to their deaths.

This mantle starts working on the called one in the next generation who is willing to pay the price and live a life that allows God to trust him or her with it. The one chosen by the Lord to carry the mantle must learn how to work with it both in the natural and in the Spirit. That process of preparation takes time and a diligent pursuit.

But there comes the time when the mantle begins to work through the one called to carry it, and it gradually becomes a force that cannot be stopped. And every time the mantle transfers according to God's plan to the next generation, it increases in some degree of power or scope.

**There comes the time when the mantle
begins to work through the one called to carry it,
and it gradually becomes a force
that cannot be stopped.**

Chapter 17

'FOLLOW ME, AS I FOLLOW CHRIST'

Whatever God has called you to do during your life on the earth, you will have to make choices along the way that determine how well you fulfill that call. For one thing, you must know how to follow someone.

This is an important lesson that every believer has to learn. It is especially critical for one called to inherit a mantle.

You may say, "I don't follow people; I just follow Jesus." No, you do follow someone besides the Lord, whether it's your pastor, a spiritual parent, or a mentor. It's the way the Church works.

There are certain individuals I am following, and there are people who are following me. For instance, I follow Brother Hagin, even though he's in Heaven now. I still listen to his teachings to keep my foundation strong.

Following people who follow the Lord is a vital part of Christianity. It's part of how we are inspired and instructed in the Body of Christ. We are to follow those the Lord connects us with as they follow Him.

Of course, the individuals we follow don't replace Jesus in our lives, and they don't sit in the first seat of our hearts. That is where the Lord alone sits. But somewhere along the way, someone comes across your path that you are being influenced by, and you begin to follow that person as he or she follows the Lord.

Following people who follow the Lord is a vital part of Christianity. It's part of how we are inspired and instructed in the Body of Christ.

This is scriptural, and Paul even instructed us to do it. He wrote the Corinthian church, "Follow me as I follow Christ" (*see* 1 Cor. 11:1). But Paul's instruction implied this: "*Don't* follow me if I'm *not* following Christ."

You must understand *how* to follow a person in the Lord before you actually commit to it. You must look at that person's life. I would suggest this: Of those who are already in Heaven, follow only people who did well all the way to the end. And as for those who are on the earth, just make sure that the individual is following the Lord so you can trust the process and follow him or her to learn, to receive, and to become better equipped.

In this process, you must learn not only how to follow someone, but also when *not* to follow someone. If a leader takes a doctrinal detour or falls into sin, you are not to follow that person down the same wrong road. If you do, you're in danger of stumbling into the same trap or the same sin that the leader fell into.

This, then, is the lesson that many called to carry a mantle over the years have failed to understand. Following someone correctly is not an easy thing. The disciple has to know how to follow the leader without picking up weaknesses or repeating past mistakes.

Too often in past generations, those called to carry a mantle missed that point in following their leader. They didn't stay alert for warning signs when their senior started to consistently make scriptural errors or moral mistakes. They followed too closely, picked up on the mantle carrier's problems, and ultimately fell into the same ditch.

The bottom line is this: You have to know how to follow someone *as that person follows the Lord.*

The bottom line is this:
You have to know how to follow someone
as that person follows the Lord.

COMMON PITFALLS OF THE HEALING MANTLE

Let's go back for a moment to the national healing mantle we just discussed. That level of a mantle is a powerful responsibility. We've seen that each one who carries it will have a strong ministry that gets national attention. Each one will become a dominant leader in the Church. And each one will face great opposition designed to throw them off course.

That means the successor of such a mantle needs to study the enemy's strategies in previous generations. That kind of knowledge will prepare him or her to follow the one who came before correctly and avoid falling victim to the same types of demonic strategies. This is so important, because Lucifer assigns a demon prince to each one called to carry such a mantle, with cooperating powers sent to buffet him or her.

For instance, I'll highlight here two of the distinct ways the devil fights this national healing mantle: First, every single one of those called to carry that mantle experienced great marital challenges that led to divorce.

As we discussed, Mother Etter went through a divorce in the 1890s after her husband ran off and had an affair with another woman. Aimee went through divorces with her second and third husbands. As for Kathryn, her only big mistake in her life was that she married a man who was handsome and had an outwardly respectable ministry but who lied to her to get what he wanted. That marriage also ended in divorce.

In addition, each of the women of this generational healing mantle died from conditions in which heart problems were a contributing factor.

Those assigned to carry this mantle in subsequent generations may have a great anointing, but they will have to know the devil's strategies in order to avoid his traps. In particular, they will need to be careful to guard their marriage and their heart health, because the enemy hates this healing mantle that came to Kathryn, who received it from Aimee, who received it from Mother Etter. He wants to hurt the one who carries this mantle, and he'll look for a way to get in.

**Those assigned to carry this mantle
in subsequent generations may have a great anointing,
but they will have to know the devil's strategies
in order to avoid his traps.**

I am emphasizing these common threads of how the enemy fights this particular healing mantle because it's such a vivid example. It should alert future successors to discern patterns of attack so that the same type of attack doesn't happen to them. When one called to inherit a mantle recognizes that certain demonic strategies are possible, that gives the successor a certain posture of watchfulness to stay aware and to deal with any issues before the situation gets too serious.

WHY SOME MINISTERS DIE EARLY

Let me take this thought a little further, because this principle impacts every person called to the ministry who is serious about accomplishing the purpose he or she has been put on the earth to fulfill. Every minister who wants to run his race well and finish strong has to learn to walk in God's wisdom in every area of life, and that includes staying alert to the enemy's tactics.

For instance, one reason some ministers graduate to Heaven earlier than they need to is that they built their faith for the operation of their gift, but neglect to build faith for themselves. The second reason is they don't take care of themselves. Ministers who closely follow someone who is making one or both of these mistakes are susceptible to making the same errors in their own lives if they're not careful.

One reason some ministers graduate to Heaven earlier than they need to is that they built their faith for the operation of their gift, but neglect to build faith for themselves. The second reason is they don't take care of themselves.

If ministers violate natural laws long enough, they will get sick. If they allow the sickness to become chronic, it could lead to death. Aimee McPherson and Kathryn Kuhlman are two examples. If those two ministers had slowed down, they possibly could have lived longer. But they loved God, and they loved what they were doing. They had set a pace early, and they didn't want to slow down.

You see, when you're in the Spirit, you're never tired! And when you're in the anointing a large part of your time, you can almost lose contact with your natural body. Then when you finally stop long enough to be aware of how your body is doing, you can almost be shocked: "How did I get sick?"

You see, the anointing can act like a drug — a minister can get addicted to it if he isn't careful. He or she has to learn how to live with the anointing and operate in it with wisdom, or it can cause problems.

Ministers who have a difficult time coming out of the anointing can cause family problems. So many don't know how to "be home" and be the parent. Many men who are ministers don't know how to be a dad to their children — go fishing with them, play baseball with them, etc. — because they are always "in the anointing." Some preachers may have been better off if they had never gotten married and just stayed in the anointing, because they have made family a second or third priority in their lives, and it has created problems.

Many people just assume that natural crises don't happen to ministers, but ministers face life just like everyone else does. They are not exempt from the storms of life. The key lies in how well they walk in God's wisdom to prevent avoidable problems and to face any storm that does come their way. And for those who are married, husband and wife need to face the storms together as partners in life and not allow the pressure to pull them apart.

SOMETIMES IT'S KNOWING WHEN TO STOP

At times a person has to learn when to *stop* following another. I'm thinking of a minister who is a good man of God but who became fixated on the prosperity message years ago in the wrong way. His overemphasis on that one theme developed as he followed another minister who also made that mistake. In the end, the collapse of this minister's church was almost identical to what happened to the ministry he followed.

This minister became too fixated on teaching a particular truth. Whenever that happens, the truth that is being over-emphasized is taken to the extreme and becomes an error.

When you see that type of error happening in someone's ministry, you need to take heed and stop following that person. If you stay on board, you will cross over and become a casualty when all the stupid stuff starts — whether it's bad doctrine, a wrong choice, an excess in wrong behavior, etc. You have to stay alert and recognize if a leader begins to get off-balance in certain areas so that you don't follow him or her right into a ditch.

How do you avoid making this kind of mistake? You must pursue a person not by the soul, but by your *spirit*. When you do that, you pick up on the right qualities in that person's life and ministry and your spirit will help you avoid whatever is off-balance or wrong.

This is such an important principle for every person to learn, but it is especially important for one called to fulfill the responsibility of a mantle assignment. Why is this? Because every person has something that God is working on adjusting or eliminating from his or her life.

So even as you follow and receive from a leader's ministry, you have to know that God is still working on him or her. No one ever reaches perfection. Even if a leader lives to be 100 years old, God is still at work from the inside out to help mature, train, and equip His child. That's just part of living life in Him.

You must pursue a person not by the soul, but by your spirit. When you do that, you pick up on the right qualities in that person's life and ministry and your spirit will help you avoid whatever is off-balance or wrong.

FOLLOW ELISHA'S EXAMPLE

As we discussed in Chapters 5 through 8, Elisha is a biblical example we can look to of one called by God who accurately followed his elder. Elisha pressed through years of pursuit and serving to ultimately receive the double portion. That is the often-challenging path of one called to inherit a mantle. But there is also a spiritual principle here that applies to whatever purpose God has called a person to fulfill.

I want people to follow Elisha's example. I want them to have whatever God wants them to have. I don't want them to pick up on error that will take them off track.

Brother Hagin used to tell us to follow people like Brother Wigglesworth. Wigglesworth didn't make many mistakes. You can follow him all of his life, and you won't have to worry about picking up on the wrong thing.

Follow people like Oral Roberts, Kenneth Hagin, and Kathryn Kuhlman. It's true that Ms. Kuhlman experienced a marriage and divorce that should never have taken place. But she fixed that mistake and never repeated it again. Yes, you can learn from her relatively early death how to better pace yourself for longevity. Nevertheless, you will do well to follow Kathryn Kuhlman for most of her life.

You can follow people as they follow the Lord and receive the blessing, the graces, and the joys of their anointing and obedience. But if you're following someone who took a wrong direction and ended up in a ditch, you better know *where* the wrong turn occurred and *why* it happened so that you know when to stop following that person.

Chapter 18

CASE IN POINT: WILLIAM BRANHAM

...It was amazingly demonstrated in the Louisville meeting that the sick can be healed en masse by the Gift of Healing. Brother Branham ventured on this procedure there, inviting those on cots, those in wheelchairs, and the crippled to be brought forward first, and then those who could walk on their crutches and those suffering with cancer and other diseases to come toward the front and stand behind the stretchers and wheelchairs.

As they began to surge forward, their faith began to pull on the healing virtue in the gift, and the healing demonstration was beyond anything yet witnessed in a Branham meeting. While on their way forward, Brother Branham pointed rapidly to one after another saying, "Christ has healed you." The people threw their prayer cards into the air, threw down their crutches and those who could not stand or walk sprang to their feet, some of them jumping and praising God for joy. The demonstration was beyond description.[25]

HUMBLE, YET SUPERNATURAL BEGINNINGS

Regarding this principle of knowing when to stop following someone, I want to share from the life and ministry of William Branham as a case in point.

Branham was very possibly the greatest modern prophet in the last several hundred years, considering that his level of prophetic gifting seemed akin to one of the prophets of Bible times. Yet Brother Branham started out as a simple hillbilly country man from Kentucky. His mama and daddy, Charles and Ella Harvey Branham, were just teenagers when he was born in 1909 in a one-room log cabin with one window near a town called Burkesville.

The day William was born, his parents laid him in his little homemade crib. Soon afterward, they saw a perplexing sight: a ball of fire in the woods, moving through the trees and heading for their cabin.

The couple stood there at the small window and watched the ball of fire for a while as it journeyed toward them. When it reached the log cabin, the light came through the window into the house; then it moved to the crib and set upon the little baby.

That's how God told Branham's parents he was called to be a man of God. They were uneducated, and they understood signs

---

[25] Gordon Lindsay. *William Branham: A Man Sent From God* (Revival Library. Kindle Edition), p. 156.

like that. So that's how God spoke to them — in a "language" they understood.

When William was about eight years old, his mother sent him down to the nearby creek with a bucket to get some water. On his way to the creek, a wind blew through the branches of a nearby tree — whoosh! — yet young William noticed that all the other trees stood still. He stopped to look at the unusual sight. There it was: One tree was moving around with the wind, and the tree next to it wasn't even budging.

As William stood there, out of that wind a Voice came, saying: *"Do not smoke or drink or defile your body when you're older. I have a work for you to do."*

That scared little boy Branham! He dropped the bucket and ran back to the house, crying, "Mommy, a tree talked to me!" William's mother thought that he had just gotten frightened by a wind blowing through the trees. She told him to go lie down and take a nap to calm himself; then she walked down to the creek and got the water herself.

DIVINE VISITATION

That was the first time William heard God's voice in his life. But the divine visitation that defined his life and ministry occurred in 1946. Branham was home in bed when he noticed a light flickering in the room. Thinking someone was coming with a flashlight, he looked out the window but saw no one. Suddenly the light began to spread across the floor. God had dispatched an angel to leave Heaven, go to Branham's home, and walk down the hallway into his bedroom.

William saw the feet of a man coming toward him. As he continued to shift his gaze upward from the feet, he saw a man standing before him who appeared to be about 200 pounds in weight, clothed in a white robe. Then the angel said these words to William: *"Fear not. I am sent from the presence of Almighty God to tell you that God has sent you to take a gift of divine healing to the peoples of the world..."*

Branham's first response was much like Gideon's (*see* Judges 6). William told the angel that he was poor and uneducated and that no one would accept his ministry or listen to him. But the angel continued, *"You will be given two gifts by God. From this night forward, they shall be active, and they shall be upon you and within you."*

The two gifts given to William Branham that night were to know the secrets of men's hearts and to perform signs and wonders by the anointing of God so that men and women might believe in Jesus Christ and in Branham's message from Heaven. The angel went on to tell Branham that if he would be faithful to his call, the results would reach the world and shake the nations.

Then the angel said these words to William:
"Fear not. I am sent from the presence of Almighty God to tell you that God has sent you to take a gift of divine healing to the peoples of the world..."

As for William, that angelic visitation was a shock to him. At that time, Branham was actually more Baptist in his thinking, although he had intersected with the Pentecostals over the years. When it came to the Holy Spirit, William Branham didn't know much more about Him than His role in convicting the heart of man.

William was first introduced to the Pentecostals when he was a young Baptist minister. He was driving down the road one morning in 1936, and he saw a tent meeting in progress at the side of the road. Curious, he pulled off and entered the tent just as the minister was finishing his sermon.

It was a "Jesus only" Pentecostal tent meeting, and after the sermon, the director got up and announced, "We've decided to ask the youngest preacher under the tent, whoever he is, to preach this afternoon." As it turned out, the youngest preacher was Branham, and he wasn't even a part of their group!

When the Pentecostal leaders found out William Branham was the youngest, they told him, "You get to preach this afternoon!" Brother Branham was quite reluctant. He didn't think he was dressed well enough for the honor in that unfamiliar environment, but eventually he was persuaded to preach. When it was time, William got up to speak — and the Holy Spirit swept in as he preached a fiery message.

These "Jesus only" Pentecostals immediately picked up on William Branham's anointing, even though he had yet to understand it. After Branham's message, he received multiple invitations to come preach at different churches. But when he arrived back home, William listened to other people's counsel and backed off from working with the Pentecostal world until after his 1946 angelic visitation.

SIGNS AND WONDERS!

That heavenly visitation was the line of demarcation for William Branham. From that point on, he stepped into his call as a prophet, and signs and wonders began to follow. Branham is credited with being God's appointed catalyst who helped usher in the powerful Healing Revival, which began in the late '40s and lasted through most of the '50s.

Branham's associate in ministry, the renowned healing evangelist F. F. Bosworth, provided an eyewitness account of those early years of William Branham's prophetic ministry. Bosworth worked with Branham during that time period and had witnessed the extraordinary power of the Holy Spirit operating through him, just as the angel had declared in that 1946 vision. And even though F. F. Bosworth had spent more than 30 successful years bringing the miraculous healing power of God to the multitudes himself, he still wrote with great conviction, "I have never seen or read of anything to equal the healing ministry of William Branham."[26]

That heavenly visitation was
the line of demarcation for William Branham.
From that point on, he stepped into his call
as a prophet, and signs and wonders began to follow.

---

[26] Gordon Lindsay, *William Branham: A Man Sent From God* (Revival Library, Kindle Edition), pp. 147.

Bosworth went on to relate the miraculous demonstrations he had witnessed in William Branham's ministry after Branham's 1946 angelic visitation:

The first sign: When the Angel appeared to Brother Branham, he told him how he would be able to detect and diagnose all diseases and afflictions; that when the gift was operating, by taking the right hand of the patient he would feel various physical vibrations or pulsations which would indicate to him the various diseases from which each patient was suffering.

Germ diseases, which indicate the presence and working of an "oppressing" (Acts 10:38) spirit of affliction can be distinctly felt. When the afflicting spirit comes into contact with the gift, it sets up such a physical commotion that it becomes visible on Brother Branham's hand, and so real that it will stop his wristwatch watch instantly. This feels to Brother Branham like taking hold of a live wire with too much electric current in it. When the oppressing spirit is cast out in Jesus' Name, you can see Brother Branham's red and swollen hand return to its normal condition.

If the affliction is not a germ disease, then God always reveals the affliction to Brother Branham by the Spirit. This first sign usually raises the faith of the individual to the healing level; but if not, the second sign does.

The second sign: The Angel told him that the anointing would cause him to see and enable him to tell the suffering many of the events of their lives from their childhood down to the present time. He even tells some their thoughts while they are coming to the platform or before they came to the meeting.

I heard him say recently to a mother bringing her little girl, "Lady, your child was born deaf and dumb; and as soon as you discovered she could not hear, you took her to the doctor," and then he told the mother exactly what the doctor said. The mother said, "That is exactly right."

The great audience hears all this over the public address system. Brother Branham actually sees it enacted, and pushing the microphone away so the audience won't hear it, he tells the patient any unconfessed and unforsaken sins in their lives which must be given up before the gift will operate for their deliverance. As soon as such persons acknowledge and promise to forsake the sin or sins thus revealed, their healing often comes in a moment before Brother Branham has time to pray. These statements by the Angel are verified in the Branham meetings nightly before the eyes of thousands.[27]

Over the years as I researched William Branham's life and ministry, I personally interviewed people who sat in his meetings during those powerful early years of his prophetic healing ministry. They all said that Branham was in himself a plain-spoken, rather boring preacher. But then the miracles would begin, and the people would all come to attention. This was why the crowds packed out Branham's meeting venues — for the miracles. And every single one of the individuals I interviewed made this statement: William Branham never missed it when he was operating by the Spirit in his giftings.

Brother Branham was so precise in the operation of his prophetic gift that he often could tell a complete stranger his name, address, and phone number! When Branham arrived for a meeting and an usher opened his car, he would start talking to the usher with knowledge of that usher's personal details as if Branham had been with him all day long. Branham might talk about the restaurant the usher had eaten at, what the usher's wife was doing that day, how each of his children were doing,

---

[27] Ibid., pp. 149-150.

and what the doctor had recently said to him. And that was just from the car to the back door of the church!

In Branham's meetings, there was often an "Elijah-level" degree of dramatic miraculous demonstrations. For example, one time the Branham team was holding a crusade in Phoenix, Arizona, and the power of God hit the platform. The piano player fell off the bench, and the piano kept playing — and this was back before there were electronic keyboards that can be programmed to play without a person! It was the real thing! That's just one example of some wild signs and wonders that would happen in the ministry of William Branham.

BRANHAM'S SHIFT INTO ERROR — AND THE CONSEQUENCES

In those beginning years of Brother Branham's prophetic healing ministry, he did well. He not only had F. F. Bosworth, but also Gordon Lindsay working with him. Both were solid, anointed teachers of the Word, and they would do the preaching for him. Then Branham would get up and minister in the gifts of the Spirit, and miracles would start happening.

That was good spiritual order. If Branham had stayed in his lane, everything would have continued to be wonderful. But in the latter 1950s, Brother Branham made a fateful misstep that many others in the ministry have also fallen prey to over the years: *He decided he wanted a gifting that God didn't grant him.* He thought he could change offices at will, and he wanted to be a teacher.

So many times people make this same mistake to their detriment. They decide they want to do what others are doing more than what God has called *them* to do.

William Branham made that mistake. He was an amazing prophet, but he chose to start operating in the wrong office and then got into error. In the end, Branham died early, thinking he was Elijah. That was the same deception another of the great Pentecostal leaders, John Alexander Dowie, eventually fell into during the early years of the 20th century.

If Branham had stayed in his lane,
everything would have continued to be wonderful.
But in the latter 1950s,
Brother Branham made a fateful misstep
that many others in the ministry
have also fallen prey to over the years:
*He decided he wanted a gifting
that God didn't grant him.*

I respect Brother Branham's prophetic ministry tremendously. But I learned by studying his life that those who follow this particular minister better know when to stop following, or they will get sidetracked.

A person can't operate in a ministry office if God didn't give that office to him. God alone is the One who decides that.

Branham was a powerful seer, a healer, and a "signs and wonders" man, but he was *not* a good Bible teacher. My question to William Branham would have been this: "You can read some-one's mail in detail and then get that person healed! God uses you to perform amazing miracles of healing and deliverance. So why would you want to try to expound on Bible doctrine, when He has appointed teachers to do that so beautifully?"

Nevertheless, toward the end of the healing revival in the latter 1950s, Branham saw in the Spirit and prophesied about the teaching movement that was to be birthed in the coming years. Then he decided that *he* wanted to be a teacher — period. His own will became more important than God's call, and that's when he started down a wrong path.

Branham began trying to teach, but so much of what he taught wasn't just slightly off — it was actually goofy. I'll give just one example of Branham's teaching to illustrate the bigger picture. He would say, "Whenever you go to a funeral, you can know it's a woman's fault." His theology behind that assertion was that Eve ate the apple and caused the Fall — and as a result, all consequences of the Fall are the woman's fault.

Now, that is not at all correct theology or teaching. But William Branham had attained great influence among the general population throughout the nation because of all the signs and wonders that occurred in his meetings. Many people therefore just assumed that whatever Branham said must be true, and they unquestioningly swallowed his "revelations." People didn't judge everything by the Word, and it got them in trouble.

Years passed, and William Branham kept changing offices at will. He was especially causing trouble among the Pentecostals, because many weren't well established in the Word. They didn't know that someone's gifts may be working beautifully, yet that person could simultaneously be teaching error. They believed if a minister was that accurate when operating in the gifts of the Spirit, everything he said and did could also be trusted. And by the thousands, people began to believe Branham's wrong doctrine.

Branham kept going down this wrong road for several years, until God eventually had a problem with him staying on the earth. God's people were being led astray as Branham got further and further off in his doctrine. Eventually the time came when God's hand of protection was lifted off him, and Branham went on to Heaven early.

This was one instance when the Spirit of the Lord allowed the destruction of someone's flesh for the saving of the soul (*see* 1 Cor. 5:5). God in His love took a man of God so he wouldn't keep hurting the Church and so that *he* wouldn't go to hell, because error in its height is hell-bound if it keeps going that way. I know that is a tough statement, but it's true. It happens rarely, but it happens.

The error William Branham was producing and the damage it was causing in the lives of so many had to stop. Branham had made a choice, and he just would not change. He wouldn't listen to people he had previously listened to — people who were only trying to help him.

Soon after Christmas in 1965, Branham was in a car with his wife Meda, driving from Arizona to Indiana, when a drunk driver suddenly hit their car head-on. Branham's son and family were caravanning in a car in front of them. When his son saw what happened in the rearview mirror, he immediately turned their car around, parked, and ran to his parents' car.

I talked to this son years later, and he related to me what happened next: "I went over and checked Mom, and she was dead. There was no pulse, no breath, no movement. She was gone. Then I came over to my dad on the driver's side. His condition was bad; he was conscious but could barely just whisper.

"Dad asked me, 'How's your mom?' I answered, 'Dad, she's gone.' He said, 'Put my hand on her' — because he was so injured that he couldn't move his hand on his own. I picked up his hand and laid it on Mom's knee. My dad closed his eyes — and in about a minute, Mom opened hers. She came back to life!"

**Branham had made a choice,
and he just would not change.
He wouldn't listen to people
he had previously listened to —
people who were only trying to help him.**

So William Branham's last miracle was raising his wife from the dead, but he himself died soon afterward.

You may say, "Well, that's a very sad story." Yes, it *is* very sad. But these types of tragedies keep happening all over the world. Doors to the enemy are opened when people don't listen to wise counsel and refuse to change their rebellious internal attitudes to obey God's Word and follow *His* path for their lives.

THE DANGER OF FOLLOWING ERROR

Branham's death didn't stop the error with some of the most zealous "Branham-ites." They continued to follow him as if he were still alive. Some people still go to this day to Branham's grave every Easter in case he might be raised from the dead. That's how crazy it is.

The young prophetic generation of today often hear only of the beauty of Branham's prophetic gift; then they start trying to be a bunch of "Branham juniors." Those who do this are engaged in a pursuit born of self-will, not of the Holy Spirit's wooing.

I get asked about Branham's story all the time by people in this category, but I never hear this question: "Did Branham make a mistake?" They don't want to hear that. They want to hear about the angels and the glowing vapors — the spectacular side of his story.

When I teach about William Branham's mistake, people who follow Branham often don't respond that well. "I don't like that part," they say. But no one actually has a right not to like it, because it's the truth! They need to open their eyes and see his story from Heaven's perspective.

People who still follow Brother Branham want to partake of his supernatural ministry. I'm not against that — but people have to know when to stop following him. They can follow him right up to the time in his life when he chose to become a teacher; then they must remove themselves from that pursuit. Not one teaching from that day forward should they listen to. They must inquire very little about his life after that date so they can stay on the correct side of his story.

Remember, the Apostle Paul said, "Follow me *as I follow the Lord*" (*see* 1 Cor. 11:1). Paul didn't just say, "Follow me forever, no matter what." His words imply this: "As long as I am following the Lord, follow me. Should I ever stop following Him in any area, stop following me."

This is so important to understand when you're working with God in this world of anointings, impartations, and mantles. How you follow is greatly significant for the stability of your future.

When people follow William Branham, they have to stop at a certain year — somewhere around the mid-1950s — or they put themselves in danger of getting off in their belief system the way he did. Some folks tried to make everything Branham said to be a prophetic dream or a new revelation, yet many things he taught were just stupid and wrong. People who follow Branham to this day might say, "How dare you touch the anointed!" But I have no trouble touching wrong doctrine to keep people from following someone into a ditch!

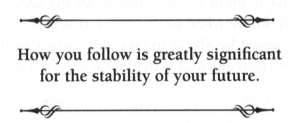

**How you follow is greatly significant
for the stability of your future.**

I love Brother Branham. I think he was a wonderful prophet in his early years of ministry. I look forward to talking to him when I get to Heaven. But we can't follow him past the point of his obedience to his call. For all the young prophets of today who are following after William Branham without this understanding, goofiness and weirdness shall be their testimony.

Knowing when to stop following guarantees a healthier life in ministry. And to stop following someone because he or she has stopped following God in some area is not disrespect, nor is it yielding to a demonic suggestion. You are not coming against anything. You have simply determined, "This is not according to Scripture. I therefore stop right here and follow no further."

We have to know when to stop following someone. If we don't, God's plan will be delayed still further as we start down a wrong path and influence others to do the same.

We have to know when to say *yes* to this and *no* to that. We cannot be afraid to take the correct stand in the heavens and articulate it on the earth!

"Well, people will get mad." They're already mad — so let's get anger going in the right direction! *Oh, we cannot lose this moment in time through fear of man!*

**We have to know when to stop following someone.
We have to know when to say *yes* to this and *no* to that.
We cannot be afraid to take the correct stand
in the heavens and articulate it on the earth!**

GIVE HONOR WHERE HONOR IS DUE — BUT NO MORE

Those whom God is calling to carry a mantle have a destiny in this next hour to preach, to lead, to train, and to carry His miraculous power into the earth. But they must pursue that call with wisdom so their influence on this earth will not shrink and disappear.

So if you are sensing an alert in your spirit that it's time to stop following a leader, pay attention.

Also, don't yield to sentiment that wants to take you down memory lane. "Oh, but it was so great in those days." I'm a church historian, so I listen to all sorts of people as I collect the stories of God's generals. But I refuse to live back in the time those generals lived. I will go wherever they lived to learn and ask and receive, but I'm not living in what *was*. I'm living the *what is* and *what is coming*!

I don't tell the stories of the lives of God's generals just as a part of a historical record. I tell them because if you can learn from what they did right and wrong, you can be better in *your* day! You don't have to become "Branham crazy" to be "Branham good." It is not a lack of honor to know when to stop following!

True Honor

There is actually a famine of true godly honor in the Body of Christ. Too often it's one of two extremes: On one hand, there is a lack of respect or honor for the minister of God. He is just "one of the guys." People don't receive who he is in Christ or how God set him in the Body.

On the other extreme, people can give too much honor. This error doesn't get talked about a lot, but I've seen people who were being given too much honor in different places of the world and it bothers me.

I refuse to live back in the time those generals lived.
I will go wherever they lived to learn and ask
and receive, but I'm not living in what *was*.
I'm living the *what is* and *what is coming!*

The Apostle Paul allotted by the Spirit the maximum honor we are to give to the greatest among us. Paul wrote to Timothy about it, giving instruction that those who work in the Word and prayer were to be given double honor — no more and no less (*see* 1 Tim. 5:17-18).

If people begin to exceed that amount of honor for their leader, they can easily get into idolatry. Idolatry begins when people set a minister on a pedestal beyond where God wants that minister to be. Then thieving starts as ministers begin to take glory for themselves that belongs only to God.

Ministers can sometimes do that by mistake. When that happens, they will sense in their spirits that they have grieved the Holy Spirit and will be able to adjust themselves.

The problem is that some ministers like triple or even tenfold honor. But there are two things God does not share with any human: *vengeance* and *His glory* (*see* Rom. 12:19 and Isa. 42:8). So when someone goes after more than double honor, that person is in trouble. He or she is stealing from the Most High.

People asked Kathryn Kuhlman one time, "How do you stay so happy?" They expected her to answer with some deep spiritual truth. But this is what she said: "Jesus allows me to receive just enough thank yous to stay encouraged for one day. All the rest of them go to Him, to whom they belong."

I think that's a beautiful way to state that. Double honor is the max. God will give minister some time to come to their senses. But taking more honor than a person should is addictive to the human personality. Those who refuse to listen to the warnings of the Holy Spirit can lose the very anointing that caused the attention in the first place. The anointing will go dormant or wane if they continue to refuse to humble themselves and listen to the Lord, and they could possibly even die early.

This takes us back to the beginning of this discussion in the previous chapter. It's an example of a time when a person must know when to *stop* following so that he or she doesn't fall into the same ditch. As Brother Hagin used to say, it makes all the difference in the world whom you follow. Your destiny could depend on it.

As Brother Hagin used to say,
it makes all the difference in the world
whom you follow. Your destiny could depend on it.

Chapter 19

PASSING ON A MANTLE: NAVIGATING THE TRANSITION

I do believe there are mantles in Heaven waiting for those called to carry them to do what is necessary to pick them up. I also believe there are new mantles specifically for these end times that God wants to bring to the earth. And, finally, I believe there are mantles God has already put in the earth that lie dormant, waiting for the next one called to carry it who is willing to pay the price.

Sadly, not every mantle finds a qualified successor; some mantles actually lie dormant for generations. That isn't God's intent, but it has happened at times because of people's ignorance or wrong choices and an enemy bent on thwarting the plan of God on the earth.

WHY MANTLES SOMETIMES GO DORMANT

The enemy has always looked for ways to sabotage a smooth transition of succession between generations. The advantage we have in this present generation is the ability to learn from the lessons Scripture provide for us so we avoid the same pitfalls.

**Sadly, not every mantle finds a qualified successor;
some mantles actually lie dormant for generations.
That isn't God's intent, but it has happened
at times because of people's ignorance
or wrong choices and an enemy bent on
thwarting the plan of God on the earth.**

We can see this principle played out regarding God's intended line of succession for Elijah's mantle (*see* Chapters 5 through 8). After Elisha, the mantle became an example of one that wasn't passed on to the next generation because of the intended successor's wrong choices.

In 2 Kings 13, we read about a dead man being raised to life when his lifeless body touched Elisha's bones because of the power of the mantle that still resided there. I used to preach on this biblical account only as a great miracle of God's resurrection power — and it was certainly that. But it's also a sad story when we consider the reason that there *was* enough power resident in Elisha's bones to raise the man from the dead.

> **And Elisha died, and they buried him. And the bands of the Moabites invaded the land at the coming in of the year. And it came to pass, as they were burying a man, that, behold, they spied a band of men; and they cast the man into the sepulchre of Elisha: and when the man was**

let down, and touched the bones of Elisha, he revived, and stood up on his feet.

2 Kings 13:20-21

The mantle that the prophet Elisha carried in life had no place to be transferred at his death. It was still stuck in the earth and in the bones of the man who had last inherited it. And when some men burying a dead man were interrupted by danger approaching, they quickly put the corpse into the most convenient grave at that moment. But to their surprise, they encountered one of God's suddenlies!

Those men had never conceived the possibility of what was about to happen. They were simply looking for the nearest grave to deposit the dead man's body and then escape from the Moabite band coming to kill them. But when they threw the man's corpse on top of Elisha's bones, the mantle was still active and powerful, and the man was raised from the dead!

I personally believe that the mantle was supposed to pass on to Elisha's servant Gehazi, but he failed to qualify. As a result, the last reference in Scripture of this mantle in operation is this account of the dead man being raised to life from Elisha's grave.

So people read that and say, "Wow, that's a great story! The anointing was there in Elisha's bones!" But it's actually a sad testament to the lack of qualified recipients to inherit the mantle in the next generation.

God doesn't want His mantles stuck in the graves of the last generation! Too many mantles over the centuries got stuck in weird places and today still lie dormant because those whom God called to inherit the mantles in succeeding generations wouldn't pay the price to qualify for the position.

God doesn't want His mantles
stuck in the graves of the last generation!

GEHAZI, THE WEAK LINK
IN THE SUCCESSION LINE

In the case of Elijah's mantle, I believe Elisha's servant Gehazi may have been the reason that mantle had nowhere to land after Elisha's death. Perhaps it was Gehazi who was destined to receive the mantle from Elisha as he had received it from Elijah. But if that's the case, Gehazi aborted that process at a crossroads moment when he revealed his own selfishness and deceit.

That moment came on the other side of one of the greatest miracles of Elisha's ministry. A general in the Syrian army named Naaman was afflicted with leprosy. At the suggestion of a Jewish handmaiden who served his wife, Naaman eventually found himself in the presence of the prophet Elisha, asking for help. The full story can be found in 2 Kings 5, but it is enough here to simply say that Naaman was miraculously healed of leprosy when he obeyed the prophet's instructions.

We will pick up the story in verse 17, where Naaman asked Elisha what he could do to show his gratitude for his healing. Elisha's response was simple and selfless: "Go in peace."

But soon after, Gehazi failed his own personal test of character. He wasn't willing to let this opportunity to enrich himself pass him by.

> And Naaman said, Shall there not then, I pray thee, be given to thy servant two mules' burden of earth? for thy servant will henceforth offer neither burnt offering nor sacrifice unto other gods, but unto the Lord. In this thing the Lord pardon thy servant, that when my master goeth into the house of Rimmon to worship there, and he leaneth on my hand, and I bow myself in the house of Rimmon: when I bow down myself in the house of Rimmon, the Lord pardon thy servant in this thing.

> And he said unto him, Go in peace. So he departed from him a little way. But Gehazi, the servant of Elisha the man of God, said, Behold, my master hath spared Naaman this Syrian, in not receiving at his hands that which he brought: but, as the Lord liveth, I will run after him, and take somewhat of him.

> So Gehazi followed after Naaman. And when Naaman saw him running after him, he lighted down from the chariot to meet him, and said, Is all well? And he said, All is well. My master hath sent me, saying, Behold, even now there be come to me from mount Ephraim two young men of the sons of the prophets: give them, I pray thee, a talent of silver, and two changes of garments.

> And Naaman said, Be content, take two talents. And he urged him, and bound two talents of silver in two bags, with two changes of garments, and laid them upon two of his servants; and they bare them before him.

> And when he came to the tower, he took them from their hand, and bestowed them in the house: and he let the men go, and they departed. But he went in, and stood before his

master. And Elisha said unto him, Whence comest thou, Gehazi? And he said, Thy servant went no whither.

And he said unto him, Went not mine heart with thee, when the man turned again from his chariot to meet thee? Is it a time to receive money, and to receive garments, and oliveyards, and vineyards, and sheep, and oxen, and menservants, and maidservants? The leprosy therefore of Naaman shall cleave unto thee, and unto thy seed for ever. And he went out from his presence a leper as white as snow.

2 Kings 5:17-27

Gehazi's failure to pass God's test of character stands as a warning to all of us. If we want to fulfill the purpose for which God put us on this earth, we would do well to take heed.

In my early years of ministry, I had some team members working for me whose different character issues I had seen in the beginning. However, I thought those character flaws had been repented of and dealt with because their behavior had changed consistently for the better as they worked for me over a period of time. However, I discovered later after our paths parted and these team members left to go another direction that they had regressed back to dealing with those issues once more.

I learned through those experiences that some character flaws do not get resolved in a person's life until he truly makes a decision to work on overcoming that sinful area once and for all. This is where the role of a spiritual father is so valuable — one who is willing to cross the boundary and enter into the spiritual son's private life to deal with character flaws that will sabotage his call if those issues aren't dealt with.

Gehazi's failure to pass God's test of character stands as a warning to all of us. If we want to fulfill the purpose for which God put us on this earth, we would do well to take heed.

Sometimes without a spiritual parent, that aspect of a person's fleshly makeup hides and goes dormant because it's intimidated and afraid in the presence of authority. That's what happened in the case of my former team members, and I believe that's what happened with Gehazi. This covetousness and materialism was lurking in Gehazi all along. But he wasn't fooling God, and he wasn't fooling Elisha. The prophet could see by the Spirit behind the front that Gehazi presented.

Notice that Elisha didn't say, "We shouldn't have what Naaman is offering." He just said, "It isn't the time for it."

So there was a truth Naaman and the Syrians had to understand at that moment: that God does good out of love and compassion, not out of expectation of payment. And Gehazi also had a lesson to learn. He needed to know that just because God does something great through one of His servants doesn't necessarily mean that His servant has earned a material reward. God will take care of His people, but sometimes the bigger Kingdom principle overrides personal benefit or desires.

I also see this situation as a test for Elisha's servant. God was watching to see what Gehazi would choose to do in this situation. This is especially true if Gehazi was being trained to inherit that prophetic mantle.

**This covetousness and materialism
was lurking in Gehazi all along. But he
wasn't fooling God, and he wasn't fooling Elisha.
The prophet could see by the Spirit
behind the front that Gehazi presented.**

Gehazi could have responded when Elisha confronted him about what he had done, "I did receive Naaman's gift for myself. I'm sorry; I repent! Please help me."

King David did that. And even though David suffered for his sin, he repented. He threw himself on the mercy of God, and God forgave him. And still today David is known as a man after God's own heart and the great king of Israel.

So I believe that if Gehazi had thrown himself on the mercy of God and of the prophet, he may have gotten a second chance. But Gehazi didn't repent when Elisha confronted him, and in the end, he was disqualified.

I believe Gehazi also had a pride issue that kept him from repenting — because if a prophet "reads your mail" and tells you all about the sin you've been trying to hide, the only thing you need to do in that moment is cry out, "Have mercy on my soul! I'm wrong, and you're right. God of Israel, help me!" But Gehazi didn't do that.

Gehazi appears once more in Scripture when the king of Israel summoned him into his presence to tell him more about Elisha's ministry. It's important to note the strategic timing of this meeting, for God used the information Gehazi provided to set up another blessing in the life of the Shunnamite woman who had honored and obeyed the words of the prophet Elisha during his years of ministry (*see* 2 Kings 4:18-37).

It came to pass at the seven years' end, that the woman returned out of the land of the Philistines: and she went forth to cry unto the king for her house and for her land.

And the king talked with Gehazi the servant of the man of God, saying, Tell me, I pray thee, all the great things that Elisha hath done. And it came to pass, as he was telling the king how he had restored a dead body to life, that, behold, the woman, whose son he had restored to life, cried to the king for her house and for her land. And Gehazi said, My lord, O king, this is the woman, and this is her son, whom Elisha restored to life.

And when the king asked the woman, she told him. So the king appointed unto her a certain officer, saying, Restore all that was hers, and all the fruits of the field since the day that she left the land, even until now.

2 Kings 8:3-6

Most scholars believe this was the same Gehazi who was judged at the healing of Naaman. Some believe that the timeline of 2 Kings is not linear and that Gehazi's audience with the king came before Naaman's healing.

However, theologian Adam Clarke helps resolve the question this way:

This is supposed to have happened *before* the cleansing of Naaman, for is it likely that the king would hold conversation with a leprous man; or that, knowing Gehazi had been dismissed with the highest disgrace from the prophet's service, he could hold any conversation with him concerning his late master, relative to whom he could not expect him to give either a true or impartial account?

Some think that this conversation might have taken place after Gehazi became leprous; the king having an insatiable curiosity to know the private history of a man who had done such astonishing things: and from whom could he get this information, except from the prophet's own confidential servant? It agrees better with the chronology to consider what is here related as having taken place *after* the cure of Naaman. As to the circumstance of Gehazi's disease, he might overlook that, and converse with him, keeping at a reasonable distance, as nothing but actual contact could defile.[28]

Whether or not Gehazi was advising the king before his judgment at the healing of Naaman, I believe the conclusion remains the same: Gehazi had messed up and gotten cut off from his inheritance in the prophetic lineage. That judgment not only affected him personally, but also those still to be born in his family line. Disqualified from receiving the mantle, Gehazi's wrong choice possibly ensured that the power resident within that mantle would lie dormant for many, many generations to come.

However, as I said earlier, I do believe it's possible that we who are alive today will be the generation to witness the rebirth of many mantles that have lain dormant too long. These mantles

[28] Adam Clarke, *Clark's Commentary*, 2 Kings 8:4, https://www.studylight.org/commentaries/eng/acc/2-kings-8.html.

are just waiting for those who are both called and qualified to hear the call and pay the price to pick them up.

Gehazi had messed up and gotten cut off
from his inheritance in the prophetic lineage.
That judgment not only affected him personally,
but also those still to be born in his family line.

ELI, HIS SONS, AND SAMUEL

The account of the prophet Samuel's life is a scriptural example that reveals how the enemy works to sabotage the succession of a divinely appointed position between one generation and the next. Thankfully, Samuel's story also reveals the hand of God at work to provide His replacement so His plan for man could continue to unfold.

Hannah, later to become Samuel's mother, was a woman of Israel whose greatest desire was to give birth to a child. Her husband Elkanah was also married to another woman named Peninnah, who had given birth to several children. Still, the Bible makes it clear that Elkanah's first love was Hannah:

> ...Whenever the time came for Elkanah to make an offering, he would give portions to Peninnah his wife and to all her sons and daughters. But to Hannah he would give a double portion, for he loved Hannah, although the Lord had closed her womb.
>
> **1 Samuel 1:4-5 NKJV**

Hannah's rival Peninnah continually provoked her, taunting her about her barren womb. So when the family traveled to the house of the Lord at Shiloh on their yearly journey to offer sacrifices for their sins, Hannah drew aside and went before the Lord alone at the altar to ask Him for a child.

Eli, who was both the priest of Shiloh and the judge of Israel, was sitting in his seat near the doorpost of the tabernacle, watching over everything that took place (*see* 1 Sam. 1:9). Eli observed Hannah as in bitterness of soul, she "...prayed to the Lord and wept in anguish" (v. 10 NKJV).

Not having a child was a matter of great trauma to Hannah. Verses 10-11 (NKJV) relates her agonized prayer to the Lord:

And she was in bitterness of soul, and prayed to the Lord and wept in anguish. Then she made a vow and said, "O Lord of hosts, if You will indeed look on the affliction of Your maidservant and remember me, and not forget Your maidservant, but will give Your maidservant a male child, then I will give him to the Lord all the days of his life, and no razor shall come upon his head."

As Hannah prayed before God, Eli saw that her lips moved but her words were not voiced because it was so deep and so personal.

You may have seen an example of what Eli saw when people are praying at the church altar. Sometimes you can tell that someone is silently and intensely talking to God about a private, painful matter.

Eli had stood in the office of priest and judge of Israel for many years, but on this day he came to a wrong conclusion regarding what he saw. Thinking Hannah was drunk, he spoke up to correct her.

> And it happened, as she continued praying before the Lord, that Eli watched her mouth. Now Hannah spoke in her heart; only her lips moved, but her voice was not heard. Therefore Eli thought she was drunk. So Eli said to her, "How long will you be drunk? Put your wine away from you!"
>
> But Hannah answered and said, "No, my lord, I am a woman of sorrowful spirit. I have drunk neither wine nor intoxicating drink, but have poured out my soul before the Lord. Do not consider your maidservant a wicked woman, for out of the abundance of my complaint and grief I have spoken until now." Then Eli answered and said, "Go in peace, and the God of Israel grant your petition which you have asked of Him."
>
> **1 Samuel 1:12-17 NKJV**

In the months that followed, Hannah's prayer was answered. Soon she gave birth to an infant son and named him Samuel. A few years later, she returned to the tabernacle of the Lord and, true to her word, dedicated her son to God's service.

> Now when she had weaned him, she took him up with her, with three bulls, one ephah of flour, and a skin of wine, and brought him to the house of the Lord in Shiloh. And the child was young.
>
> Then they slaughtered a bull, and brought the child to Eli. And she said, "O my lord! As your soul lives, my lord, I am the woman who stood by you here, praying to the Lord. For this child I prayed, and the Lord has granted me my petition which I asked of Him. Therefore I also have

lent him to the Lord; as long as he lives he shall be lent to the Lord." So they worshiped the Lord there.

1 Samuel 1:24-28 NKJV

Once a year after that, Hannah would travel to the temple to visit her son, and every year she would bring him a new robe that she had made for him (*see* Joshua 2:18). She had given her son to the Lord's service, but she was still being a mom. And she was happy about this arrangement. That says something strong about Hannah's godly character and the power of her prayers for her son.

TROUBLE BREWING IN THE HOUSE OF GOD

God's plan was in place. Samuel was a called one being prepared as he grew up in the service of the Lord before Eli. Meanwhile, a drama was playing out in Eli's household that wasn't going to end well. God knew that Israel would have need of a righteous leader in the days ahead.

Now Eli was very old; and he heard everything his sons did to all Israel, and how they lay with the women who assembled at the door of the tabernacle of meeting. So he said to them, "Why do you do such things? For I hear of your evil dealings from all the people. No, my sons! For it is not a good report that I hear. You make the Lord's people transgress."

1 Samuel 2:22-24 NKJV

Eli heard what his sons, Hophni and Phineas, were doing. He heard how they were seducing women to have sex with them in the tabernacle of God, perhaps convincing gullible women that it was part of their act of worship. But the father's feeble correction fell on deaf ears. Long before that moment, Eli's sons had learned to close their ears to their father's correction. It was too late to fix the problem. Hophni and Phineas were hell-bent to go the way of rebellion.

Samuel was a called one being prepared
as he grew up in the service of the Lord
before Eli. Meanwhile, a drama was playing out
in Eli's household that wasn't going to end well.
God knew that Israel would have need
of a righteous leader in the days ahead.

But God had a plan in motion. He still wanted a successor to the father — a man called to stand in that office as judge of Israel.

Meanwhile, verse 26 (NKJV) shows the contrast between Eli's rebellious sons and Samuel's obedience before the Lord:

And the child Samuel grew in stature, and in favor both with the Lord and men.

Young Samuel was growing up right there in the house of these two disobedient sons, yet they couldn't see that God had already cut them off and sent a new successor.

A barren woman had made a vow to the Lord, and God had replied, "So be it. I will honor your request." Then she honored Him back for His kindness and gave her son to the work of the Lord to be raised in the temple.

The boy Samuel grew up in the temple, helping Eli in practical ways — simple chores such as lighting the candles in the tabernacle, running errands, and cleaning. Yet even as Eli taught Samuel in the ways of righteousness, the elderly father was failing to rein in his own rebellious offspring.

Eli's sons continued to commit grave sin and bring reproach on the priesthood and the name of the Lord. Meanwhile, Samuel was growing up in favor with God and man.

God had blessed the young boy with the beginnings of an anointing as he obediently busied himself around the temple. As a result, people favored him. They probably came into the temple asking, "Where is that little boy Samuel, Eli? I like him. He always runs around with such a happy disposition." Many who came to the tabernacle to worship probably gave Samuel little gifts out of affection.

Eli's sons continued to commit grave sin and bring reproach on the priesthood and the name of the Lord. Meanwhile, Samuel was growing up in favor with God and man.

But one night the voice of the Lord visited young Samuel, and everything changed.

THE WORD OF THE LORD RESTORED

First Samuel 3:1 (NKJV) says, "...And the word of the Lord was rare in those days; there was no widespread revelation."

Before that night, there had been no moving of the Spirit or word of the Lord during the entire time Samuel grew up in the house of God. There had been no open visions, and the heavens stayed closed because of the weak leadership of Eli and his failure to deal with the sin of his sons.

> **And it came to pass at that time, while Eli was lying down in his place, and when his eyes had begun to grow so dim that he could not see, and before the lamp of God went out in the tabernacle of the Lord where the ark of God was, and while Samuel was lying down, that the Lord called Samuel. And he answered, "Here I am!" So he ran to Eli and said, "Here I am, for you called me." And he said, "I did not call; lie down again." And he went and lay down.**
>
> **Then the Lord called yet again, "Samuel!" So Samuel arose and went to Eli, and said, "Here I am, for you called me." He answered, "I did not call, my son; lie down again." (Now Samuel did not yet know the Lord, nor was the word of the Lord yet revealed to him.)**
>
> **1 Samuel 3:2-7 NKJV**

Twice Samuel went to the room where Eli slept and answered what he thought was Eli's call. Twice Eli sent Samuel back, because it wasn't the priest's voice that Samuel heard.

> **And the Lord called Samuel again the third time. So he arose and went to Eli, and said, "Here I am, for you did call me." Then Eli perceived that the Lord had called the boy. Therefore Eli said to Samuel, "Go, lie down; and it shall be, if He calls you, that you must say, 'Speak, Lord, for Your servant hears.'" So Samuel went and lay down in his place.**
>
> **1 Samuel 3:8-9 NKJV**

The boy returned to his room, got back in bed, and lay his head back down on his pillow. Soon that voice came again: *"Samuel, Samuel."*

This was all new for young Samuel. The only one who had ever called his name before that moment was Eli. So Samuel had the natural reaction; he ran again to Eli and said, "Yes, I'm here. What did you need?"

Finally, Eli realized that it was the Lord speaking to Samuel. It took this priest and judge of Israel three times to recognize that God was in the church! That's how dull and out of tune to the Spirit of God Eli was!

As the priest leading Israel, Eli was supposed to be quick to see, hear, and discern what was happening. But he had back-slidden in his office as a result of disobeying God with his own sons, so it took him awhile to finally recognize what was happening: *The Lord is talking to young Samuel! I thought He would only talk to me and my boys...*

That's why the word of the Lord was rare in those days. I'm sure God had wanted to do something in those latter years of Eli's life. But Eli had become so used to responding to situations in the natural that he didn't recognize the moment when God intervened and had something to say.

The Bible talks about Eli's eyes waxing worse in verse 2. Eli couldn't see much of anything anymore — but that also described the state of his spiritual eyes. It wasn't just Eli's advanced age that was his issue; it was the condition of his spirit.

Eli had become so used to responding
to situations in the natural that he didn't recognize
the moment when God intervened
and had something to say.

A Divine Transfer of Succession

So Eli finally said, "Samuel, I perceive that it's the Lord who is calling you" (*see* 1 Sam. 3:8).

Until then, Eli had mostly given Samuel natural duties and not much spiritual work. But the ministerial training began in earnest in that moment. Eli told Samuel, "When you hear that voice, if it comes again, that is the Lord wanting to reveal something to you. Here is how you respond to Him: You just say, 'Speak, Lord, Your servant hears.' That's all you say, and then you listen."

I don't believe young Samuel went back to sleep after he got back in his bed. We don't know how much time passed, but eventually that Voice came again: *"Samuel... Samuel."*

The Lord has a way of saying your name that says a whole lot more than just your name.

When the Lord said, *"Samuel,"* His voice ignited the awakening of the anointing and the gifting in Samuel — the opening of his spiritual ears and eyes to be a prophet.

"*Samuel...*" Then the waiting to see if Samuel would respond the right way. The boy answered, "Yes, Lord, your servant hears." Notice Samuel didn't say, "Your young servant" — he simply said, "Your servant hears."

When the Lord said, "*Samuel,*" His voice ignited the awakening of the anointing and the gifting in Samuel — the opening of his spiritual ears and eyes to be a prophet.

The long silence between Heaven and earth had ended, but it wasn't Eli's sons God was communicating with — it was the barren woman's son. This was Eli's tragic confirmation that the prophecy he had earlier received from a prophet was true.

> Then a man of God came to Eli and said to him, "Thus says the Lord:… 'Did I not give to the house of your father all the offerings of the children of Israel made by fire? Why do you kick at My sacrifice and My offering which I have commanded in My dwelling place, and honor your sons more than Me, to make yourselves fat with the best of all the offerings of Israel My people?'
>
> "Therefore the Lord God of Israel says: 'I said indeed that your house and the house of your father would walk before Me forever.' But now the Lord says: 'Far be it from Me; for those who honor Me I will honor, and those who despise Me shall be lightly esteemed.
>
> "'Behold, the days are coming that I will cut off your arm and the arm of your father's house, so that there will not be

an old man in your house…. Now this shall be a sign to you that will come upon your two sons, on Hophni and Phinehas: in one day they shall die, both of them. Then I will raise up for Myself a faithful priest who shall do according to what is in My heart and in My mind. I will build him a sure house, and he shall walk before My anointed forever.'"

1 Samuel 2:27-31,34-35 NKJV

According to the word of the Lord, Eli's succession line had undergone a divine transfer. In the midst of the spiritual mess within Eli's home, God had brought little Samuel in from the outside, and he would be the one to later succeed Eli as judge of Israel after his death. The hand of the Lord had been removed from Hophni and Phineas and was now upon the young lad.

**According to the word of the Lord,
Eli's succession line had undergone
a divine transfer.**

God may have desired the succession of this position as leader over Israel to have continued through the biological line, but it wasn't to be in this case. Samuel was brought into the mix through the spiritual connection made at the moment of a mother's vow before the Lord (*see* 1 Sam. 1:11). And when the time came for Hannah to give her little boy into the care of Eli, she was able to say, "I have kept my bargain. God gave me a son, and I gave him back to Him. Please train my son Samuel in the service of the Lord." Thank God, she was a woman who kept her word!

So Samuel grew up helping Eli in any way he could, sitting at the feet of the elderly priest to learn. The young boy was watching everything going on around him, asking questions and listening intently as Eli spoke of the past mighty acts of God, the principles of judging the people, etc.

Meanwhile, Eli's sons were out sinning with weak-willed women — missing their hereditary call, missing the anointing for their lives, sacrificing their purpose for existence. All of these eternal treasures were being indifferently swallowed up and discarded for earthly, fleeting pleasures.

SAMUEL'S FIRST PROPHETIC ASSIGNMENT

God told young Samuel on that night when everything changed that it was the end of Eli's house. What a first word of the Lord to receive! And then this young boy was charged with delivering that difficult prophetic word to Eli, the one in authority over him!

The next morning at breakfast, Eli knew the Spirit of God had been in the house, and he asked the boy, "Samuel, what did the Lord say?"

I'm sure young Samuel felt a bit of reservation about speaking out the difficult message that had been given to him to relay to Eli. Nevertheless, the boy was obedient and told Eli all that he had heard: "The Lord said that the line of priesthood and leadership over Israel in your family will end with you. Your sons have been cut off, and your family heritage has ended because their sins were not restrained."

And Eli, knowing it to be the truth, replied, "You have heard from the Lord. So be it as it was spoken" (*see* 1 Sam. 3:18).

The chapter ends with a profound statement about Samuel:

So Samuel grew, and the Lord was with him and let none of his words fall to the ground. And all Israel from Dan to Beersheba knew that Samuel had been established as a prophet of the Lord. Then the Lord appeared again in Shiloh. For the Lord revealed Himself to Samuel in Shiloh by the word of the Lord.

1 Samuel 3:19-21 NKJV

That's the way that Samuel's prophetic mantle came to him — through his obedience to tell the father of the young successors, "It's over. You have all disqualified yourselves." And everyone throughout Israel knew it to be true.

People can tell when someone has the call of God upon his life. That call is working in that person, no matter what he or she is doing, and people begin to pick up on it even before there is a clear, outward demonstration of that gift. That's the way it was with young Samuel — all because of the barren woman who said to the Lord, "Give me a child, and I'll give him back to You."

As the years passed and Samuel grew toward manhood, the people's estimation of Samuel grew as well as they recognized God's favor on his life. As for the spiritual gifts that Eli's sons should have inherited and the authority of Heaven they should have had carried, these treasures continued to grow in young Samuel. He was God's chosen recipient of the mantle of Eli's office, and it was evident to all from the time that Samuel was still a young boy.

That's the way that Samuel's prophetic mantle
came to him — through his obedience
to tell the father of the young successors, "It's over.
You have all disqualified yourselves."
And everyone throughout Israel knew it to be true.

ANOTHER 'MISS'
IN GENERATIONAL SUCCESSION

There is another profound, yet sad lesson to learn from
the life of Samuel and his family. For all that Samuel did right
throughout his life as a righteous prophet and judge of Israel, he
made one major error that hearkens back to what we discussed
in Chapter 17. Samuel followed Eli too closely in one area, picking up on his elder's weakness and repeating Eli's mistake in his
own life: Samuel allowed his sons to stray and sin against the
Lord.

Remember, when you follow someone, you are not to follow so closely that you pick up on that person's weaknesses and
mistakes.

As a result of the dishonest practices of Samuel's sons, the
people of Israel became discontent with the status quo of their
leadership. Against the Lord's counsel, they insisted on choosing a king to lead them during Samuel's lifetime.

**Now it came to pass when Samuel was old that he made
his sons judges over Israel. The name of his firstborn was**

Joel, and the name of his second, Abijah; they were judges in Beersheba. But his sons did not walk in his ways; they turned aside after dishonest gain, took bribes, and perverted justice. Then all the elders of Israel gathered together and came to Samuel at Ramah, and said to him, "Look, you are old, and your sons do not walk in your ways. Now make us a king to judge us like all the nations."

1 Samuel 8:1-5 NKJV

For all that Samuel did right throughout his life
as a righteous prophet and judge of Israel,
he made one major error: Samuel allowed his sons
to stray and sin against the Lord.

Notice that the people of Israel didn't have faith for another "miracle son" like Samuel showing up on the scene to replace the disobedient natural sons. The previous generation had said, "God will give us a spiritual leader who will follow in His ways." God had answered their prayers. They saw that the right person was being prepared to succeed Eli.

But the next generation, when faced with the same type of issue, in essence said, "No, we don't believe it. We don't have faith for it. Give us a king like other nations." So the Israelites chose the natural, carnal solution.

God warned Israel, "If you choose a king, he will take your sons for himself, and they will die on the field of battle for him. He will take increase from your fields and your vineyards for himself" (*see* 1 Sam. 8:10-18). But the people didn't have faith for God to supply another miracle son to continue the father-and-son order. So the Israelites entered the world of kings, which was God's permissive will, not His perfect will for His people.

Think of it: These sons were engaging in defrauding God's people while living in the home of the number-one prophet of the land! Samuel's sons had eaten at his table and walked with him in God's tabernacle ever since they were young. From his sons' earliest remembrance, they had heard the word of the Lord going forth and had witnessed the cloud and the fire of God's glory. These two sons of Samuel had been taught the words and the ways of God all their growing-up years — yet as adults, they still chose to live like dishonest sons of the devil, swindling God's people for their own selfish gain.

**The people didn't have faith for God
to supply another miracle son to continue
the father-and-son order. So the Israelites entered
the world of kings, which was God's permissive will,
not His perfect will for His people.**

People sometimes think, *If I could just see the glory cloud, it would change everything.* But a person seeing the glory cloud doesn't in itself change that person. Obedience to God is still a choice. The consuming fire, the sound of God's voice, the tangible sense of His presence — all of these were part of daily life for both Eli's and Samuel's sons. Yet they still chose to live like those who had never been taught the ways of God.

The outcome of Eli and Samuel's children is what I call a prophetic problem. In Scripture and in church history, it is more common that prophets don't deal with their children correctly than with other ministry offices.

But if you stand in any ministry office, I want to urge you to give special attention to your children. Don't just let the years pass with you being so focused on what you are pressing toward in ministry that you can't see what is in front of you in your home.

It is the same old problem that repeats itself again and again through the generations right up to the present day. Ministers become so consumed in the work of the ministry that they fail to spend the necessary time with their children to deal with any problems that might crop up. Therefore, the problems don't go away; they just get bigger as the children grow into adulthood. Left undealt with, those problems can grow into huge issues that bring remorse, sorrow, and shame on their entire house. Those same issues can even become the cause of God's purposes aborted for that generation of the family line.

Whether you're called to the ministry or to be God's representative in another arena of society, it would behoove you to learn from the error of Eli and Samuel. You may have set your home in order when your children were young. But as your children grow older, you must work to make sure that the order in your home doesn't gradually deteriorate until it is ultimately lost.

Cultivate a close relationship with your children, but never sacrifice your righteous standard in the home in order to "keep the peace." It's up to you to make sure your home *stays* in order.

AVOIDING FAULTY ASSUMPTIONS

Following this scriptural principle is so important for many reasons, one of which is the generational succession of divine assignment. Scripture reveals that God sometimes calls natural families to work together on an assignment from Heaven from generation to generation in the operation of what could be called "family mantles." Abraham, Isaac, and Jacob certainly demonstrate this principle (*see* Genesis chapters 12-50).

**Cultivate a close relationship with your children,
but never sacrifice your righteous standard
in the home in order to "keep the peace."
It's up to you to make sure your home stays in order.**

I believe that a family mantle can manifest not only in a multi-generational line of a fivefold ministry gift assignment, but at times also in specific professions within the secular realms of society. Throughout the centuries, for instance, there have been certain families that have produced, from generation to generation, a line of influential leaders in education, in medicine, in the arts, in the military, in government, etc.

Yet there have been time periods throughout the centuries when a generational mantle can lie dormant and, as a result, the demonstrations of the Holy Spirit's anointing become less frequent and strong. This gap in generational succession has often resulted from the backslidden state of the people God had to work with during that time period. As a result, He didn't have those whom He could trust to carry His anointing if He turned up His power.

That's why there has been a lull at times between mantle activity or generational greatness in God. For instance, after a season of great spiritual generals, the next generation sometimes simply assumes that their parents' mantle was passed on to them, regardless of whether or not they paid the same price of pursuit that the previous generation did.

God does use families, but not in violation of His own spiritual laws. Spiritual assignments are not bequeathed merely by natural family heritage. Family members must find their place in His plan first, according to their individual calls and giftings; then they must be willing to do what is necessary to qualify for their part.

However, many times the children and grandchildren of great generals in the Kingdom haven't seemed to understand this principle. This is one reason why mantles may skip a generation or two — because of the foolishness and presumption that often prevails after a general dies.

I'm not trying to judge anything, nor am I saying this happens in every case. I'm just saying that this is sometimes what happens, and time reveals everything.

And let me add this — I love it when I see the generational transfer within a ministerial family actually operate correctly! I can think of several examples of families in the Body of Christ who have successfully navigated the succession of assignment between the generations. One of the most well known of these success stories is the Osteen family of Houston, Texas.

When John Osteen, founder and pastor of Lakewood Church, went home to be with the Lord in 1999, it was his youngest son Joel who assumed the position of leading the church. There were many naysayers in the beginning, wondering how the church would fare under the leadership of young Joel, whose giftings differ somewhat from his father's. But Joel Osteen has proven that he was the one called to take the helm of that ministry assignment for this time. The church remains on course and has exploded in growth over the years since that generational succession took place.

I also believe it's important to make this point: People often assume that only one person is called to receive someone's mantle. But I believe that God will sometimes raise up more than one possible successor, because not everyone He calls will do what is necessary to qualify. As we discussed earlier, a person has to be willing to follow for a long season of preparation before receiving this kind of assignment.

Preparation in most people's minds is a waste of time, but it is actually invested time for a more secured, successful future.

I was one of those who thought that God simply selected the successor to a mantle — that it was a predetermined decision by Him alone, independent of man's choices or actions. I thought that when a mantle carrier died, God just proclaimed,

"This mantle goes to So-and-so!" — and *boom*, the mantle then fell on the appointed one!

That's how I assumed it always worked. And I have certainly witnessed instances where God declared the succession of a mantle, and it came to pass just as He said because that person was faithful to pay the price of preparation.

**Preparation in most people's minds
is a waste of time, but it is actually invested time
for a more secured, successful future.**

But over the years, I've also noticed times when God surprised everyone. There have been instances when a called one who proved faithful to diligently pursue Him and to closely follow the mantle carrier was the person who actually became the successor instead of God's first choice. So I've had to allow the Lord to adjust my simplistic explanation of how He determines the successor to a mantle.

So much depends on the heart motive behind a person's pursuit. So much rests on the strength of that person's passion and commitment to fulfill the assignment.

And even though we're talking about the succession of mantles in this discussion, this spiritual principle is true no matter what God has called you to do in this life. You will find that certain individuals cross your path, often unaware that something in their spiritual makeup sparks something in you. You will learn through these relationships that certain aspects of your anointing and your calling will not operate unless there is the pursuit of what those relationships offer that opens them.

As I said, this is true regardless of the arena of life a person is called to excel in — but it is certainly true of those who are called to carry a mantle.

So much depends on the heart motive behind a person's pursuit. So much rests on the strength of that person's passion and commitment to fulfill the assignment.

THE GENERATIONAL SUCCESSION OF MOSES TO JOSHUA

There is much we can learn from Joshua chapter 1 about God's way of navigating the succession of an assignment from one generation to the next. Joshua was the one whom God had called to one day take Moses' place as leader of the Israelites. And after the days appointed for the people to mourn Moses' death, the Lord gave Joshua a clear message.

> **Moses My servant is dead. Now therefore, arise, go over this Jordan, you and all this people, to the land which I am giving to them — the children of Israel.**
>
> **Joshua 1:2 NKJV**

When someone is succeeding another, the statement, "Moses My servant is dead," is not a disrespectful one; it is simply a fact. It is also a statement to initiate action, because God was saying to Joshua, "Now it is time for the next leader to move the people forward!"

God was dislodging any improper loyalty of the soul in the people. He knew it would hinder the proper progression from the former anointing of the last generation to the anointing of the new generation. People often don't want to let go of the familiar bond formed over the years with the previous leader to lay hold of what God wants to do with His new leader.

Moving on after a leader or mantle carrier dies is *not* the equivalent of cutting off that leader's ministry or of saying there is no more value to receive from him or her. Thank God, that leader pioneered and labored for the Kingdom! There is great spiritual wealth to be gleaned from the truths he or she imparted while on the earth. But the Lord is always wanting His people to move forward, building upon the foundation laid by former generations during their mandate on the earth.

Too many times there is a false loyalty that people try to cling to as they try to keep everything the way it was under the former leader when he or she was alive. But there are only two ingredients of past moves that must be protected and continued into the future: *the Word of God* and *the true move of the Spirit*.

The Word will never change; the Holy Ghost will never change. The godly character of former leaders and the eternal truths learned from them as they flowed in the Holy Ghost will never change. But there will always be diversities of gifts, administrations, and operations in the Body of Christ.

In addition, all the natural things are subject to changing with the times: the music, the styles of clothing, and the methodologies. So when people try to cling to "the way it was" under a former leader when he or she was on the earth, they create a false loyalty that hinders what the Holy Spirit wants to do under the new leader in the present season.

**The Lord is always wanting His people
to move forward, building upon
the foundation laid by former generations
during their mandate on the earth.**

'Now Therefore, Arise, Go Over...'

"Moses My servant is dead," God told Joshua. "He's dead; it's over. he's not coming back." Then God continued on to show Joshua the character of his larger calling:

> ...Now therefore, arise, go over this Jordan, you and all this people, to the land which I am giving to them — the children of Israel.
>
> **Joshua 1:2 NKJV**

Notice the words *now, arise,* and *go over.* Sometimes the successor will find hints of his or her call and anointing in what others might think are obscure words that God is saying in his spirit or in a prophetic utterance. *"Now therefore, arise, go over...."* Those words encompass everything Joshua was as a leader and the nature of the assignment he accomplished in the years following that divine instruction: his entire disposition, the mighty man of valor he became, and the flow of his strategizing mindset.

Joshua arose and led the people over the Jordan River to conquer the land of Canaan. And what God said to Joshua in verse 3 took the assignment a little further:

Every place that the sole of your foot will tread upon I have given you, as I said to Moses.

Joshua 1:3 NKJV

Here we see the hereditary aspect of this call. Part of Joshua's job was to do what Moses had not done in order to complete the possessing of the promised inheritance.

We talked about this in Chapter 8 concerning Elisha, who had to finish what Elijah did not complete of the Lord's mantle assignments. Sometimes within a successor's call is the responsibility to complete what was not finished in the last generation. That won't represent the total call, but it could be a part of it, as it was with both Joshua and Elisha.

**Part of Joshua's job was to do what Moses
had not done in order to complete
the possessing of the promised inheritance.**

Then in verse 5 (NKJV), here comes the comfort of the Spirit:

No man shall be able to stand before you all the days of your life; as I was with Moses, so I will be with you. I will not leave you nor forsake you.

In the announcement of Joshua's calling, God presented His own posture with Joshua — where He stood and what He would do for him: *"I will be with you as I was with Moses. I will not leave you nor fail you — so get up, go over the Jordan, and take the land!"*

As a new leader steps into the assignment he has inherited, God will remind that leader, *"Did I not say? Did I not tell you? I'm reminding you of My past words to you..."* Why does God do that? He wants to undergird and strengthen the leader's resolve to accomplish the assignment!

New leaders can be tempted to pull back when they aren't certain God is the One leading them to take that step of faith. That's the number-one thing that hinders successors from stepping out in their calling. They lack the spiritual sensitivity that enables them to stay fully assured that they are on the right track and the presence of God is with them, no matter what the natural circumstances look like.

And this is true for all of us. Sometimes in the faith walk, we don't "feel" God's presence. All we have to step out on is the Holy Spirit's reminder to our spirits of what God has already said to us.

HOW TO LIVE
IN THE CALLING OF GOD

In the next few verses, God instructed Joshua on how to live with this divine mandate and anointing that he was about to step into as Moses' successor.

Sometimes God will give a person specific instructions that are relevant to what He has called that person to do. This is important, because in my observation over the years, certain anointings are attacked by specific types of spirits in a greater way than other anointings.

Sometimes in the faith walk, we don't "feel"
God's presence. All we have to step out on
is the Holy Spirit's reminder to our spirits
of what God has already said to us.

For instance, every minister will have to face rejection, but apostles and prophets seem to face bulldozer-sized attacks of rejection. Therefore, those called to one of those two offices must keep their spirits especially fortified with God's words of affirmation and strength in order to withstand those attacks and keep forging ahead in their assignments.

In this case, God had a message for Joshua as he got ready to assume the leadership role that Moses had once filled in order to lead Israel into the Promised Land. God started giving Joshua instructions on how to live with this anointing and fulfill his calling:

> **Be strong and of good courage, for to this people you shall divide as an inheritance the land which I swore to their fathers to give them. Only be strong and very courageous, that you may observe to do according to all the law which Moses My servant commanded you; do not turn from it to the right hand or to the left, that you may prosper wherever you go. This Book of the Law shall not depart from your mouth, but you shall meditate in it day and night,**

that you may observe to do according to all that is written in it. For then you will make your way prosperous, and then you will have good success. Have I not commanded you? Be strong and of good courage; do not be afraid, nor be dismayed, for the Lord your God *is* with you wherever you go.

Joshua 1:6-9 NKJV

Notice what God told Joshua that he had to do in order to experience good success and prosper wherever he went.

First, Joshua had to recognize that God was always with him, whether or not Joshua felt His presence (*see* v. 5).

You will have to do the same as you fulfill *your* call, whatever that may be. There are times you will have to get up and do certain things the Lord has asked you to do, and there won't be any goosebumps or nice feelings to help you do it. You will just know that He said it and, therefore, He's going to come through when you obey Him.

Then in verse 6, God started by saying, "Be strong...." That was Joshua's second instruction. In other words, God was telling him, "*Joshua, for you to do what you are called to do, you cannot love weakness. You must love strength. Every day you must seek to become stronger.*

"*Every time you feel weak, you must take time out of the execution of your leadership duties to get away with Me and find strength in My presence before you return to the people to lead them. You can only lead when you are strong, Joshua, because when you are weak, you will veer to the left or to the right, and you won't go the right way.*"

Then let's look at what God said next in verse 6 (NKJV): "...And be of good courage...." Later in verse 9 (NKJV), The Lord added, "...Do not be afraid, nor be dismayed...." All of these speak of a strong soul and of emotional maturity.

God was telling him, *"Joshua, for you to do what you are called to do, you cannot love weakness. You must love strength. Every day you must seek to become stronger."*

Where do people faint first? In the thoughts of their minds. That was what happened to the parents of this younger generation whom God was now calling Joshua to lead into the Promised Land.

Joshua had been present years earlier when those parents either saw the giants in the land or heard the ten spies' report about the giants (*see* Num. 13:21-33). He watched how the people's own thoughts about the giants caused their view of themselves to shrink to the size of grasshoppers in their own minds. And in the midst of the people's fearful thoughts, they forgot about the size of their God.

As for this younger generation, they had labored 40-some years in the wilderness. They had seen their parents die there, and many may even have lost faith themselves. So God was reminding Joshua, *"Don't let your soul lag behind in the strengthening of your physical and spirit man. Make your soul go with you, strong and steady, when you lead these people forth in strength.*

"To lead the people, you must have within yourself the ability to refuse to be dismayed. You have to stay strong, courageous, and brave, Joshua, or you won't be able to complete this assignment."

God was telling His man how to *live* in this calling. Before the challenges of the assignment unfolded, He was laying out the ground rules.

"Joshua, this is how you do it. Your earthen vessel and your soul must continually be kept strong. It is the only way you can experience the joy of accomplishment at the end of your life and be able to say to Me with confidence, 'I did what You asked me to do.'"

**God was telling His man how to *live* in this calling.
Before the challenges of the assignment unfolded,
He was laying out the ground rules.**

It's important to note that in verse 6 (NKJV), God referred to "...the land which I swore to their fathers..." as an inheritance for the people. But that inheritance wouldn't come automatically to the Israelites. They had to obey what God was commanding them to do in order to *possess* the land He had given them.

In verse 7 (NKJV), God repeated His command to Joshua to "...be strong and very courageous...." But notice that God went a little bit further, saying, "...that you may observe to do according to all the law which Moses My servant commanded you...."

In other words, God was telling Joshua, *"Do what the Book says. Live the right kind of life; pursue My ways. Don't go any other direction. Just because you're the anointed leader with whom the Spirit is found, don't think that My moral law is different for you or that you get to live by an easier set of rules than everyone else does. Everything you need, I have already given. You simply must observe My statutes — live them and pursue them."*

God continued to speak to Joshua in verse 8 (NKJV), saying, "This Book of the Law shall not depart from your mouth...." He was warning His new leader, *"You will have to watch the words of your mouth, Joshua. Don't talk about feeling like a grasshopper. Talk about how you're going to obtain your inheritance and give it to your children and your grandchildren! Keep your conversation in line with the principles of Scripture. Observe what I have said. Stay watchful and meditate on My words."*

Once again, God emphasized to Joshua the importance of keeping his soul strong and causing his mind to prosper by meditating on God's Word and bringing every thought into captivity of His truth and His ways. Then God told Joshua the outcome of his obedience: "...For then you will make your way prosperous, and then you will have good success" (v. 8 NKJV).

Notice that it was Joshua who was responsible for making his way prosperous by obeying what God had told him to do. Complete obedience to God was Joshua's only option if he wanted to experience good success. The same principle is true for the inheritor of any mantle assignment.

And the same is true for you. There is no other path to success except obedience. You cannot let negative occurrences dictate your high-call obedience. When God calls you, it's always there for you to answer!

What a sense of divine purpose and security must have been established in Joshua coming out of that supernatural experience with God! We see powerful evidence of this in Joshua's ability to immediately implement God's instructions. Joshua told the people in essence, "Pack your bags and prepare provisions for a journey — because in three days we're headed out of brown land and heading straight for green grass! We're going through the Jordan River and into the Promised Land!"

Then Joshua commanded the officers of the people, saying, "Pass through the camp and command the people, saying, 'Prepare provisions for yourselves, for within three days you will cross over this Jordan, to go in to possess the land which the Lord your God is giving you to possess."

Joshua 1:10-11 NKJV

Three days later, the Israelites headed out. Right at the onset of the journey, they experienced another "Red Sea" miracle in the crossing of the Jordan River at flood stage (*see* Joshua 3:1-17). And from there, the Israelites began to conquer the land of Canaan just as God had instructed them to do.

There is no other path to success except obedience.
You cannot let negative occurrences dictate
your high-call obedience. When God calls you,
it's always there for you to answer!

Years later before Joshua died, he was able to leave to his children the inheritance that he had received as fruit of his obedience to possess the land (*see* Joshua 24:29-30). But it is in Joshua 1:1-10 that the inception of that assignment is revealed. In these first ten verses of the book of Joshua, God included the successional transition, the announcement to go forward, the nature of Joshua's call, and how he was to live in that call. Then in verse 10, Joshua activated the assignment.

God will expect every one of His leaders, as He did with Joshua, to:

- Let go of the past and move forward.

- Stay strong and courageous, regardless of the obstacles they encounter along the way.

- Refuse to become dismayed or intimidated by anything that happens or that comes against them as they pursue their divine call.

These are the same ingredients that God will give to anyone called to inherit a mantle assignment — and for that matter, to all who are called to assume the weighty responsibility of leading His people.

Chapter 20

It's Time!

What a journey into the world of mantles it has been! And the adventure will continue beyond the pages of this book. There is more for us to learn. There is further for us to go — and we're open to learn and receive! It's time to get this subject of mantles sorted according to God's Word. We have to stay right on track with what God wants to do and *how* He wants to do it.

With that in mind, I want to summarize a few key points we've discussed along the way. We've discovered that the dominant mantle operating under the New Covenant is the mantle, or the clothing, of Christ. All of us as believers carry that mantle, and we're so thankful for it, for it is the greatest spiritual treasure we carry.

We've also seen that different forms of the Elijah-Elisha mantle found under the Old Covenant are evident in the Church under the New Covenant. So the mantle of Christ isn't a replacement of that Old Covenant mantle; it is a glorious and greater addition given to all who accept Jesus as their Savior.

We all received the mantle of Christ, and that is the primary mantle of the New Covenant. But it is evident that there are also specific and powerful mantle assignments that continue under this dispensation.

It's time to get this subject of mantles sorted according to God's Word. We have to stay right on track with what God wants to do and *how* He wants to do it.

God puts together different mighty mantles, such as this healing mantle we've been studying through three generations, to be a working militant force on the earth for His purposes. This category of mantles is still active on the earth to fulfill Kingdom assignments.

As a church historian, I have spent most of my life tracking these types of operations on the earth. And as I mentioned in Chapter 2, I've come to believe that God sometimes calls an entire church to take up a mantle assignment. Everything I've observed has caused me to conclude that a mantle can at times rest as an assignment on a body of believers rather than on one individual.

We want every one of God's strategic mantles successfully transferred to the next generation. It's not about glorifying the person. It's about a God-called individual — and at times, a God-called body of believers — standing in the authority of a mantle bestowed by Heaven. And whatever the particular mandate of that mantle, the common goal of all is to bring the demonstration of the Father's love and power to the Body of Christ and to the nations in order to further His great plan.

WHY THIS IS WORTH CONTENDING FOR

I have also observed, especially in this present season of the Church, that there is an overabundance of people looking to receive a mantle for themselves.

This book has focused on a vital and powerful reality — the mantles that must be picked up, prepared for, and deployed on the earth for this last-days move of God. As we have discussed, not everyone reading this book is destined to receive a mantle. Yet each reader must recognize the true operation of mantles on the earth and be blessed by those who are the legitimate possessors of Heaven's present-day mantle assignments.

That's the fight. That's what I'm contending for — the proper succession of Heaven's mantles. We don't want to live out these crucial last days with the Church being led by lieutenants and privates rather than God-called generals.

So to the reader who is not called to inherit a mantle, here is how you act: Thank God that these mantles are on the earth and that you have been blessed by them. Do not compete with them. Do not attack them. Bless these mantle ministries, and let them be what God has called them to be in these last days.

And to the one who reads this book and may be called to carry a mantle, here is what you must understand: You are not superior. You are merely a servant who has been given a greater measure of power for God's purposes. You are here to serve.

You are here to do what you have been assigned by Heaven. Be humbled that you were chosen, and stay determined that you will always be a faithful steward of the weighty assignment entrusted to you.

Please understand — I can only give my understanding gleaned from what I know of God's Word, as well as from what I have observed these past decades as I've sought to fulfill the ministry that God has given *me*. I'm just putting my input in the pot with everyone else. I am not trying to be the great expert who determines which one gets what mantle or the authority who specializes in "dubbing the successors."

No person is given the power to determine how the mantles that Heaven bestows are distributed. Even those who carry a mantle don't determine their successor. That responsibility is left to God. God is the One who told Elijah, "Elisha is the one." Elijah didn't choose Elisha — God did.

But it doesn't serve the Body of Christ well when lieutenants and privates are fueled by a false assumption that they belong in those seats of spiritual authority. If people pursue mantles out of their own soulish desire and not as a result of the compelling of God's Spirit, they won't have the strength of character, the depth of foundation in the Word, or the spiritual longevity to survive the environment of that position.

Individuals who fit in this category may have much to offer the Body of Christ, but their supply doesn't include the mantle they crave. The succession of a mantle is determined by God, comes at a huge cost, requires His anointing to accomplish, and requires far more than a little bit of time.

This is why the subject of the nature, function, and succession of mantles is so critical for this day we're living. The reigniting of revival is afoot on the earth. It's happening again. It's already present, and it is a beautiful thing.

The Church is beginning to rise, and God is set to move in a mighty outpouring of His Spirit! He is so ready for His people to do their part, and His Word provides the blueprint. His instructions to His man in Joshua chapter 1 are still alive to show us the way forward in *this* day.

The succession of a mantle is determined by God, comes at a huge cost, requires His anointing to accomplish, and requires far more than a little bit of time.

We are in the time of the changing of the guards from one generation to the next. There are past mantles God wants to resurrect, and there are new mantles that He wants to bring forth fresh and new in the last moments of this dispensation to finish this era and begin a brand-new era that we have never seen.

We will accomplish what God intends. And we will do it *His* way — all to the glory of God and for the accomplishing of His great plan!

Prayer of Salvation

The last days before Jesus returns are upon us, and it is critical that you make sure you are ready to go to Heaven. When you receive Jesus as your Savior, you become part of God's family.

And Jesus will never leave you. The Bible says that He is your very present Help in the time of trouble (*see* Ps. 46:1). He doesn't run from you like some people do when they get scared. In fact, when there is trouble, Jesus only gets *closer*. And if you will lean into Him, He can supernaturally fix whatever bad has happened in your life and then help make you a beautiful testimony as you walk out your new life with Him.

But the first step is to become a child of God through the sacrifice of His Son.

For God so loved the world that He gave His only begotten Son, that whoever believes in Him should not perish but have everlasting life.

John 3:16 NKJV

If the Spirit of the Lord is ministering to your heart and you want to make sure Heaven is your eternal destination, I encourage you to pray this prayer from your heart:

Jesus, I ask You to come into my life and forgive me of my sin. I receive you as my Lord and Savior, and I make a decision right now to serve You all the days of my life. I believe that I am now a born-again Christian and part of the family of God. And one day when I die, I will go to Heaven and live there with You forever!

If you just prayed that prayer for the first time, let me be the first to say welcome to the family of God!

I want to encourage you to find a good church as quickly as you can that is strong in teaching the Bible and believes in the baptism in the Holy Spirit with the evidence of speaking in tongues (*see* Acts 2:1-4). You need both the Word of God and the fullness of the Spirit of God to help you grow strong in your Christian walk. There's no time to waste. God has a prepared path and a divine purpose that you get to discover and fulfill!

But as many as received Him,
to them He gave the right to become children of God,
to those who believe in His name.
John 1:12 NKJV

PRAYER OF CONSECRATION

Is it your deep desire to hear Jesus say to you one day, "Well done, thou good and faithful servant"? If your heart says *yes*, consider setting aside a few quiet moments with the Lord to pray this prayer:

Father, I know I have a call on my life to fulfill a certain purpose — my part in God's plan — while I'm on this earth. I can't do it in my strength, Lord. I need to know Your voice and access Your power if I am going to fulfill my call the way You intend for me to do it.

So I thank You that the gift You placed in me is coming alive in a fresh way. Please forgive me for any mistakes I have made in the past in pursuing plans of my own making regarding my call and purpose on this earth. I'm so thankful that You are a Forgiver and a Restorer, that there is nothing I have done that has caused You to take Your gifts and calling away from me (*see* Rom. 11:29).

I submit unconditionally to Your will, Father. I know the path You ask me to walk is not according to my preference, but according to Your great plan. Use me for Your glory every day of my life from this day forward.

I bind every spirit of the enemy that has kept me in any type of captivity in the Name of Jesus. May the growth of my spirit and the giftings You have placed within me come alive in a greater way than ever before! I declare that I am released into my appointed domain in this world and into my call and destiny!

I thank You that You are willing to redeem any time I have lost, and I embrace a new level of momentum in my pursuit of Jesus and the power of Your Spirit.

Father, help me hunger for more of You and for Your touch of mighty power. There is no other way to fulfill what You have called me to do.

I yield myself to the Holy Spirit and allow You to work in me what is needed. You want to use me as a conduit of Your spiritual power — for Your glory and for Your love of humanity. I know there is a price to pay for that, a hunger required to obtain it, and a way to go about it — in *Your way*, in *Your time*.

So I choose to pursue You, Father, and to obey all that You are asking me to do. Day by day, I choose to receive more of You. In Jesus' Name, amen.

ABOUT THE AUTHOR

From a young age, Roberts Liardon was destined to become one of the most well-known Christian authors and orators of his generation. To date, he has sold more than 16 million books worldwide that have been translated into 60+ international languages. Roberts has ministered in 127 countries, both to the multitudes and to world leaders. He is recognized internationally and has experienced great success as a revivalist, an inspirational speaker, an author, and a church historian.

Roberts Liardon was born in 1966 in Tulsa, Oklahoma, as the first male child born to a student of the newly launched Oral Roberts University. His career in the ministry began at the young age of 12½ when he gave his initial public address. At 17, Liardon published his first book, *I Saw Heaven*, in which he related his experience of going to Heaven as a young boy. The book catapulted Roberts into the public eye and sold more than 1.5 million copies. Over the next few years, he became one of the leading public speakers in the Christian community all over the world.

When Roberts was 12½ years old, Jesus appeared to him in a vision and told him to study the great preachers — to learn both of their successes and failures. From that day on, Roberts began to devote himself to this study. This lifelong pursuit has established him as a leading Protestant Church historian, a role he carries with honor to this day.

The day came when God spoke further to Roberts about writing and producing both a DVD series and a book series entitled "God's Generals." The original mission was to chronicle the lives of some of the leading Pentecostal and Charismatic leaders so the Body could learn from both their successes and failures. The DVD series was an immediate success and became one of the bestselling Christian DVD series in the history of Christian media. The "God's Generals" book series is an ongoing assignment that also found a worldwide reading audience that has continued to grow over the years.

In 1990, Roberts Liardon moved to Southern California and founded his worldwide headquarters in Orange County. There he and his team founded Embassy Christian Center and Spirit Life Bible College, both of which became among the largest and most influential in the region.

In 2007, Roberts moved his ministry headquarters to Sarasota, Florida, where it is currently located. In 2009, he accepted the position as principal of the International Bible Institute of London, the training arm of the Kensington London City Church, a position he held for five years as an assignment from God to help further His plans and purposes for the United Kingdom and Europe.

Roberts Liardon continues to speak to this generation in pulpits across the United States and around the world. He also produces his own online courses, where he teaches on God's Generals and other key Bible truths necessary to strengthen the Body of Christ for this critical hour we live in.

Throughout the years, Roberts has continued to be a significant contributor toward building God's Kingdom, with the belief that relationships are the key element that bonds the staff at Roberts Liardon Ministries to people around the world. Each year millions are touched through this worldwide ministry, a genuine resource of victory for the entire Body of Christ.

Contact Roberts Liardon Ministries

For further information about Roberts Liardon Ministries, please visit the ministry website at
www.RobertsLiardon.org
or write us at:

U.S. Office:
Roberts Liardon Ministries
P.O. Box 4215
Sarasota, FL 34230
941-748-3883
Email: info@RobertsLiardon.org

Canada Office:
Roberts Liardon Ministries Canada
P.O. Box 800
Abbotsford, BC V2T 7A1
1-877-888-1500
Email: info@RobertsLiardon.org

UK/Europe Office:
Roberts Liardon Ministries UK/Europe
22 Notting Hill Gate, Suite 125
London WII 3JE, England
001-877-888-1500
Email: info@RobertsLiardon.org

Other ways to connect:
Facebook: Roberts Liardon Official
X (Twitter): @RobertsLiardon
Instagram: @RobertsLiardon_official
YouTube: Roberts Liardon

Equipping Believers to Walk in the Abundant Life

John 10:10b

Connect with us for fresh content and news about forthcoming books from your favorite authors...

Facebook @ HarrisonHousePublishers

Instagram @ HarrisonHousePublishing

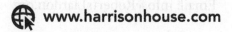

www.harrisonhouse.com

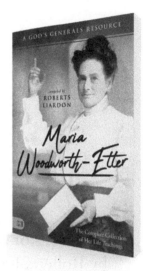
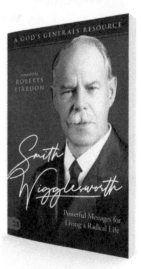

Books or other audio and video materials
by Roberts Liardon are available for purchase at:
www.RobertsLiardon.org